PASSAGE

Over the hill and around the world

Frank McNeill

Tecolote Publications

© 1998 by Frank McNeill. All rights reserved.

ISBN 0-938711-51-2

Library of Congress Catalog No. 98-60166

Printed in the United States of America

Tecolote Publications
San Diego, California

To Michael
In loving memory of his mother and my wife Janet.

To Sally & Dave 4/25/98

Hope you have a few laughs at our mistakes. Enjoy

Frank W. McNeill

Acknowledgement

I am only going to mention one very special person in this acknowledgement. There are hundreds more that deserve an honorable mention; however, I am afraid if I named any other persons, there would be many wonderful people that I would forget to mention. This special person has been my mentor, advisor, a friend who I could count on any time, day or night, to send my wife and me necessary prescriptions, medical items, and equipment replacement parts, which made our circumnavigation a success. That person is Clyde Dauben.

Contents

Foreword..1

Chapter One: Passage from San Diego, California to Bora Bora, French Polynesia..3

Chapter Two: Bora Bora to Fiji.........................26

Chapter Three: Fiji to Sydney, Australia...........37

Chapter Four: Sydney to Thursday Island, Australia....51

Chapter Five: Thursday Island to Bombay, India, via Sri Lanka..60

Chapter Six: Bombay to Israel, via Oman, Yemen, Sudan, Egypt and the Mediterranean...........................76

Chapter Seven: Israel to Skopelos, Greece, via Cyprus and Turkey..92

Chapter Eight: Skopelos to Capraia, Italy, via Athens, Cyprus, and Fumiccino, Italy.............................104

Chapter Nine: Capraia to Wesel Canal, via Monaco, Paris, and Berlin..115

Chapter Ten: Wesel Canal to Panama Canal via Netherlands, France, Spain, Portugal and Antigua.........129

Chapter Eleven: Panama Canal to San Diego, via Costa Rica, El Salvador, Mexico, and being towed home.......140

Glossary...157

History of *Isle of Barra*.......................................166

Janet and Frank McNeill......................................169

v

Foreword

For many of us our dream is to step aboard a stout vessel and take to the seas, confidently heading down the historic sea road. To fulfill just such a dream, Frank and Janet McNeill set sail westward on their forty-foot sloop, *Isle of Ibarra,* from San Diego, California, on June 11, 1983, embarking on their remarkable eleven year voyage around the world.

Throughout their voyage, many of us lived vicariously through written word and personal conversations with Frank and Janet, reading and listening to their tales of adventure, both on sea and land–personal experiences that left them exhilarated, sometimes exhausted, often frustrated through the self-absorbing power vested in the local port "official." But, at all times, the romance of the sea was evident.

Capable sailors, Frank and Janet had prepared for their voyage by sailing in several Ancient Mariner Cruises from California's West Coast to Hawaii–one time immediately after Janet had major cardiac surgery. She would, if here today, tell you that "it was nothing," and the sea journey was "just what the doctor ordered." Of course, the doctor would tell you differently.

This kind of determination bode well for them as they journeyed country to country, sometimes tarrying for weeks, months, and, in some places, years. They became tourists at every landfall; occasionally Janet found unique employment along the way. They persisted, endured, and saw all things new. And they found how freedom demands sacrifice.

The jet age is wonderful, but for the sailor the sea is the road to see the world. Here is the real-life romance of "a world that still shimmers bright as a bubble." Enjoy it while you can.

Step aboard, let go the lines, turn the wheel, and journey round-the-world with Frank and Janet McNeill.

Robert H. Smith
Del Mar, California

[Author's note: Robert H. Smith is the author of *Smith's Guide to Maritime Museums of North America and Canada* and other guides, including pleasure boat cruising for Southern and Northern California.]

CHAPTER ONE

It was just dawn. Janet and I were standing in the cockpit going over the pros and cons of shortening sail. The wind had become much stronger in the early hours of the morning and the seas were very active, probably eighteen to twenty feet. Right in the middle of our debate disaster struck. A rogue wave hit us just as a heavy gust of wind hit our sails. We estimated the wind at 50 plus knots and that was far too much. We had a knockdown. For us, a surprise of unbelievable proportions.

Both of us were pitched against the rolled down sides of our cockpit cover and we stared into the Pacific Ocean, our noses about two inches from the water. Fortunately our sails had been back winded so they didn't go very far under water and we popped right back up again. I quickly lowered our Genoa and we moved towards Maui at a much slower speed.

It is a wonder that the Genoa wasn't torn apart as it was made of 4 oz. Dacron cloth. But, in the knockdown, our SAT-NAV antenna (SATNAV is a device for electronic navigation) on the top of the mast had gone underwater which didn't help it at all. Its reaction to being dunked was to put out only hieroglyphics instead of our position on the monitor. We had received a good fix just before the knockdown so knew where we were, but from that point on we'd have to depend on my dead-reckoning to get us some 500 miles into Lahaina.

When we had backed out of our slip on the afternoon of June 11, 1983, we were beginning a circumnavigation expecting to last five to eight years. After all we weren't exactly kids. I was 62 and Janet (my wife) was 56, so we felt we couldn't spend very much time on the high seas. However, we never did feel that we were exactly geriatric. We may not have been in the prime of our age, but we were in the prime of our enthusiasm. We had gone to all the schools–sailing, navigation, amateur radio–studied diesel mechanics, and read every magazine and article we could find on sailing. We had planned this trip, in every detail, even building our own boat. After planning for more than twenty years we were, at last, going to live our dream. And we were lucky, for so many people dream and are never fulfilled. We were determined that wouldn't happen to us. We were going to sail around the world and that was that.

Our heartbeats quickened as we maneuvered out of San Diego Bay. We left at 3:00 PM on a Thursday afternoon because no one leaves then. Frankly we didn't want anyone standing on the dock waving and crying. We don't know if our leaving would have been so joyous had that happened.

As we motored past the west end of Shelter Island we looked backwards at Southwestern Yacht Club and the San Diego skyline. We knew it would be a long time before we saw them again. Just at nightfall we rounded the Coronado Islands and headed southwest for the Hawaiian Islands.

When we sailed home eleven years, one month and six days later, we were definitely members of the "over the hill"' gang. Although we were oblivious to that fact, we had to admit that we were tired and home looked very good.

The first leg of our passage was to Maui in the Hawaiian Islands. We knew how to get there–you sail about 750 miles southwest, hang a right and sail west until you're there. It is a little more complicated than that, but you get the drift. No problem, none that is except with our wind vane. Try as we would we couldn't get it to steer the boat and steering isn't one of our favorite pastimes. Not when you have to do it hour after hour.

After ten days of total frustration I announced that I was either going to get the thing to work or throw it overboard. For a long time I draped myself over the transom and watched the trim tab operation in action. Finally I shouted, "The wires are on backwards!" Tied into a safety harness, I climbed out onto the vane's supports, refastened the wires and came back into the cockpit. We reset the vane on the proper course and, VOILÁ!, it worked perfectly. What a relief. Since then we have traveled as much as six days in a row without once correcting our course by touching the wheel. As long as the wind was steady, we did not have to correct the course.

We had a few hard and fast rules that we followed. Someone was to be on duty in the cockpit at all times, standing a watch. We were quite flexible during the day. But at night I would take the 2000 to midnight and 0400 to 0800 watch. Janet would take the midnight to 0400 watch. It took about five nights in a row to get used to the strange hours. During the day if we weren't doing our specific chores we would probably be sleeping. It seemed that we could never get enough sleep.

Another hard and fast rule was that we always wore safety harnesses and always hooked on while out on deck and in the cockpit when we had a gale blowing.

We had a very expensive Ben-Mar Automatic Pilot aboard. The first time we used it our batteries dropped in voltage by an alarming degree. Therefore, unless we felt a great need for the Automatic Pilot we wouldn't attempt to use it.

On June 19, 1983, Janet made breakfast and handed me a cup of coffee as I was on duty in the cockpit. I took a sip of the coffee and immediately spewed it overboard and yelled, "Damn it Janet honey, this has got to be the worst coffee you ever made."

Naturally her feathers were ruffled. "I made it like I have always made it."

On investigation we found that a check valve in the forward water tank was defective, saltwater had entered and contaminated about forty gallons of fresh water. We knew we had plenty of fresh water on board but it made us use fresh water more conservatively.

And there was another problem–the weather. As 1983 was the year of El Niño everything was a bit strange. There was a thin yellow haze over the sky and the horizon. We couldn't see the sun, moon or stars, or anything. Using a sextant was impossible. Fortunately we had our SATNAV to give us our location, so we were never lost. We were confused a few times but never lost.

But the strangest thing during that El Niño year was that there was no sign of any life in the Pacific. We saw no birds of any kind, no dolphin or any other sea life. On two previous passages in transpac races in a small boat we had been visited by all kinds of animal life and we saw birds every day. Not in 1983. It was all rather spooky.

Also, there was no wind. So this was our slowest passage ever. We weren't making any speed at all and it was hard not to get discouraged. Then on the nineteenth day after leaving San Diego the wind finally picked up. Elated, I put up our big Genoa and we were joking about putting up the bed sheets if they'd help. At last we were moving westward at a good speed.

This is when we had the knockdown. Fortunately we didn't take very much water on board during the knock down and only a trickle splashed down the hatch which was easily cleaned up with a swipe or two of a sponge.

What wasn't so easy was to collect all the potatoes, onions, apples, citrus fruit and some boxes and cans of provisions and put them back where they belonged. Janet was taking King Neptune's name in vain, while down below cleaning up. I, being the captain, was smiling smugly to myself in the cockpit, listening to Janet's ravings. You won't believe this but after some months later there was a bad smell emanating from somewhere in the salon, getting worse as time went on. Finally we found one stinking rotting potato in a locker that was never used to put a potato in. Strange things happen at sea when you least expect it. Also water runs up hill. You figure it out, I'm not explaining it.

Periodically, and especially after a full gale or heavy weather, I will inspect every nook and cranny for loose screws, bolts, nuts, frayed lines or any damaged materials or equipment. More than one inspection turned up damaged equipment and possibly the proper maintenances we performed kept us from bigger problems. It was a lousy job, but someone had to do it.

Our boat, the *Isle of Barra*, was named after the Isle of

Barra in the outer Hebrides about ninety miles off the Scottish mainland. The Isle of Barra is the ancestral home of the Clan Mcneal. There are more than a thousand spellings of the name "McNeill."

In the beginning we made many sail changes during a twenty-four period to fit the pattern of the wind. We were getting very little sleep from having to steer and do a myriad of chores. It didn't take long to figure that it was better and much safer to make all sail changes in daylight hours, leaving the storm sails up at night. After all we were not racing and no one was expecting us in port at an exact hour.

It took 29 days for the entire passage and we both gave a sigh of relief when we finally spotted Molokai and Maui just beyond. After navigating some 500 miles by dead reckoning after the knock down and finding I was exactly on target, it gave me one of the greatest thrills of my life.

It was about midnight when the islands appeared and with my calculations we hit the Pailolo Channel right on the nose. With a limited amount of facts, dead reckoning is really a lot of guess work, so one should never rely on this method, except in emergencies. The wind died and we motored down to the Lahaina Roads and dropped anchor just to the east of the channel leading into tiny Lahaina marina.

The anchorage in the Lahaina Roads is very deep. We were in eight fathoms of beautiful clear water and could see our anchor and all the chain resting on the bottom. The sand is like concrete and your anchor never sets. So it's the weight of it and your chain that holds you in place.

A funny thing generally happens when we anchor. I always pick a spot if available at least three to five hundred yards from anyone else. Lahaina Roads is large enough to hold the seventh United States Fleet with a combination of more fleets thrown in and have plenty of room to spare. All the newcomers in private yachts felt they had to drop their hook as close to mine as possible. Then when the tides changed we would be bumping into one another. A friend of mine confided in me later that several of these yachties had asked who the grumpy old man was on the *Isle of Barra*. I would yell at them and tell them he had better up anchor and move or we would go bump in the night.

Charlie, a twelve meter boat (about 60-65 feet), a racer, had won the transpac race from Los Angeles to Honolulu and was touring Maui on a goodwill tour. Goodwill Ha! The Captain of *Charlie* anchored very close to us and then the entire crew went ashore. I was taking a nap when "Ka-boom!"–*Charlie* bumped us with such force it awakened me. At the same time Janet yelled to me for help. We called for help on our VHF radio and three young men came out in a Boston Whaler about twelve feet long. This dinghy was of heavy fiberglass construction and quite sturdy. We tossed the young men a can of beer each. They tied some life jackets on to their bow to take up the shock and stood off about ten feet. They gunned their 25 horsepower outboard and rammed *Charlie* repeatedly until the boat was quite a way off. Then they came back to us and we doled out more beer. For about an hour they kept *Charlie* off and we were running out of beer.

Finally the crew of *Charlie* came and re-anchored close to another boat whereupon they had to move again because their boat was colliding again. When Charlie was about 900 miles from Maui on the way back to the Los Angeles, we heard that their keel fell off and they had to return to Honolulu for a new one. I hope it was bad keel bolts that caused the problem and not the young men ramming into *Charlie*.

Maui is our favorite of all the islands. Perhaps due to the two previous transpac races that ended there. We made many friends there and they made our stay this time very pleasant. Thanks Suzanne for your hospitality of chablis, dining and driving us all over. We stayed off Maui for five months, sailing once up to Oahu and staying at the Hawaii Yacht Club in Ala Wai Harbor. We shopped feverishly at the US Naval Commissary, saw some doctors at Tripler Army Hospital, and then sailed back to Lahaina.

Going to and from the Hawaii Yacht Club we had a couple of passengers aboard. They were friends that we had made in Maui and we couldn't resist their plea to make the trip with us.

They were a delight to have aboard. We were very lucky, some passengers can become quite a nuisance in a very short time. We had seventeen visitors while in Maui. Not all at once, thank heavens, and only two stayed aboard the boat with us. All the rest were in various hotels on the island. We did take our usual trip to Hana and stayed in the same condominium where we always stay. As usual Hana captivated us. It is such a unique place with a 56 mile ride over what must be the roughest road in the world. But it's worth all the bumps.

Around every curve there's something beautiful to see; a waterfall, a pond surrounded by exquisite tropical blooms or full of small boys and dogs. And such luxuriant growth of bamboo and other trees and plants that it takes away your breath.

There's nothing much to do in Hana if you're looking for night life; there isn't any. I guess you have to be old folks like us just to relax and enjoy. However, there were many young people there so I'm sure they found it pleasurable there. There's just one restaurant, available only to people registered at the hotel except for Sunday morning brunch. Fortunately our condominium had a kitchen and there's a good grocery store up the hill, so all wasn't lost.

Several miles to the west of Hana is a small church and cemetery that is the burial place of Charles Lindbergh. It's a very simple grave for such a famous man who came to Maui for peace and privacy.

There was a small Episcopal church that we went to in Lahaina almost every Sunday we were there. The first time we went was nothing short of a phenomenon. When we first left our boat and got into the dinghy, a playful dolphin was gently splashing water into the boat. It seemed to know where we were going as the beautiful animal led us to the small opening in the reef, playfully splashed water on us as if to say goodbye, and left us. We went on through the reef and tied up the dinghy in the small marina, unlocked our bicycles and headed for the church.

On arriving, the smell of sweet plumaria blossoms wafted the air. Going inside we found wide drawn windows where we could still smell the wonderful aroma of the blossoms. Looking around we saw beautifully hand carved artifacts on benches–crosses, angels, you name it. Jesus himself looked every bit Hawaiian. Then two ladies came down the aisle bearing an armload of leis, placing one around the neck of every person, saying, "In Jesus' Name," and moving on to the next person. Then a short time later the Doxology was sung. A beautiful lady started the Doxology a cappella in such a beautiful contralto it brought tears to our eyes. The little church was packed and we could see the many reasons why.

As much as we loved seeing friends and touring Maui, the time had come to leave. Of all the Hawaiian Islands we visited, Maui is out favorite, and we so hated to leave, but the rest of the world was calling to us. So on a beautiful Sunday morning we raised our sails and flew down the Pailolo channel one last time. This time we were heading east for Tahiti, about 500 miles east and about 2,000 miles south of Hawaii. We had to go quite a way out to sea for the big island of Hawaii sticks out alarmingly. While our sails were full the currents kept driving us toward it. So we started up the diesel and sped on. We thought we'd never get past Hawaii and it was well into night before it disappeared from sight.

This is as good a time as any for a confession–when in the tropics and away from land, we don't wear any clothes because it is so warm. Also washing clothes by hand isn't much fun. Also on a long trip you conserve as much fresh water as possible. You never really know if you have enough fresh water. So on the sixth day out of Lahaina Janet was sitting in the cockpit wearing her wedding ring, a smile, and the earphones to our cassette player. I was below making like a Captain, writing my log, checking the barometer, monitoring the speed and such good nautical things. I finally went into the cockpit, stretched and looked around.

"My gawd! There's a ship!" I shouted.

And there was. About 300 yards away was a giant freighter flying a French flag. Janet flew down below as she heard the VHF radio calling *Ile de Barra. Ile de Barra.* As that is the name of our boat she knew that they must have used binoculars in order to see that name painted on our hull. The radioman aboard the freighter asked me if we were all right and if we needed anything. I answered "yes" to the first question and "no" to the second. Then I said, "Janet, they're leaving, don't you want to wave goodbye to them?" She replied, "Hells Bells, they were using binoculars to read the name of our boat and I'm quite sure they've seen everything else, let them wonder what the palm of my hand looks like." And we sailed on.

Two days later we saw awesome black rolling clouds ahead. We tuned into Honolulu High Seas Weather and heard them predicting light showers at that position. Within a few hours we were in the midst of the clouds and facing a full blown gale. We contacted the Pacific Maritime Net and the control asked if we wanted to speak to the weather bureau. Janet said "yes" and they dialed the phone.

When the weatherman came on line, Janet told him what he could do with his light showers. He asked, "Did we make an oops?" When told the real state of the weather he said that they'd put out a warning to mariners. Great, but a little late for us. He wanted us to report the weather to him daily. From then on the weather bureau reported the weather as we had given it that day.

When just north of the equator Janet went below to fix lunch and glanced at the SATNAV. She was horrified to see that we were 45 miles west of where we should have been. I went below and checked and agreed with her conclusion. She tuned in on the HAM radio and once more contacted the Pacific Maritime Net control. The man on the Net said that we were caught in the Equatorial Current and gave us directions to get out of it. He said we were to sail north east until free of the pull of the current, then head due south and go as fast as possible with both motor and sail to cross the current.

That we did and three days later we were across the equator and heading south on Longitude 149 degrees. We have no idea about the speed of the Equatorial Current, but it was very swift. We were running at about 5 1/2 to 6 knots and it was pushing us backwards at a steady rate. No fun at all. It was very confusing to our navigational skill.

Tahiti was just down there, about fifteen hundred miles away and the winds were now user friendly. However we did have an incredible rain storm just below the equator. It was raining so hard we couldn't see ahead. Even our bow was out of sight. We could only hope we didn't meet another boat coming the other way. Making the best of the situation, we opened up the cockpit cover, stopped up the scuppers, and filled the cockpit with fresh water. We splashed around like kids and took wonderful fresh water baths, the first since leaving Maui. A salt water bath is better than nothing, but...

After crossing the equator and the incredible rain, the rest of the sail to Tahiti was a delight with good steady winds and clear skies. As the winds were light we didn't make much speed, but plowed steadily south. Also the animal life had returned. There were hundreds of birds, dolphin and even whales.

The only surprising thing was the phosphorescence that exploded around us at night. And exploded is the right word. It was as if bathtub sized flashbulbs were going off all around the boat. Later a Tahitian friend said that was because we were too close to atolls and islands. We told him we were thirty miles from the Line Islands and he said, "That's still too close."

While we didn't make much speed on this passage, we enjoyed every minute. I caught two Mahi Mahi on different days and we had fresh fish for dinner. They were delicious. I would only fish when we needed a fish for dinner. Usually about Noon, Janet would say, "Frank, how about fish for supper tonight?" I would set the trolling pole and by two or three o'clock I would generally have a nice mahi mahi or tuna for dinner.

On the twenty-eighth day Janet was below fixing dinner when she heard me say, quietly, "Land Ho." There it was! Off our starboard side the island of Moorea appeared. Off to our left was the lower elevation island of Tahiti. The jagged peaks of Moorea were silhouetted against the sunset sky; a breathtaking sight. Every landfall is always exciting, but this one was exceptional. It was our first new territory and both of us had tears in our eyes.

We skirted the reef on the west coast of Moorea and had to

reduce sail to slow our speed. We wanted to arrive at Papeete, Tahiti, the next morning and not at night. At about nine o'clock the following morning we went through the pass in the reef and entered Papeete Harbor and dropped anchor. It was a great feeling. The day before we entered Papeete I had an attack of sciatica. I was transferring fuel from jerry jugs on deck to the main tanks. In lifting a fifteen gallon jerry jug I knew I was in trouble. Although I was in terrible pain I was still the Captain and captains have the responsibility of clearing with the officials in foreign ports. So I packed our weapons and ammunition into plastic bags, took the boat papers, our passports and launched our inflatable dinghy. I was in agony, but somehow I did it. I motored up and down the quay looking for anything that would tell me where the offices of the officials were. This was not America. This was French Polynesia. There was no flag, sign, or arrow pointing and saying, 'check in here.' Finally, in desperation, I tied to the last mooring ring on the quay.

Then, dragging the bags of weapons and ammunition behind me, I went through some barbed wire (which should have given me a hint) and entered a building nearby. The room was full of French Naval officers and personnel, many wearing sidearms, who stared at me. I asked if anyone in the room spoke English and one officer said that he did, "a little." So I told him what I wanted and the officer told me that all the official offices were closed for lunch (they take a VERY long lunch in French Polynesia) and I'd have to go later. Then he invited me to the officers's club for lunch. One more scotch and soda and I said I would not have cared about ever checking in with the officials. After being wined and dined Georges the befriending officer gave me a huge round of Camembert cheese, a bottle of red wine and sent me in a chauffeur driven car to visit the harbor police, immigration and customs. When I finished I was driven back to our dinghy and returned to our boat. My comment? "Now that's the only way to enter a foreign country!"

No pain pills seemed to help and as I was in such agony from the sciatica Janet rushed me in to see a doctor. The very busy doctor with a full waiting room, and impatient to clear out, was a little cross with us, looked at me as if to say, why is this apparently healthy looking person taking up my valuable time? Janet said, "Doctor, my husband has sciatica in his left hip and is enduring an incredible amount of pain."

Judging from his attitude, the doctor must have been thinking, "What is this woman doing, trying to tell me how to do my job?" The doctor said, "Well, you let me examine him and I'll determine if he has sciatica."

The doctor took me into an examining room and poked, prodded, and questioned me. After about twenty minutes he brought me to the waiting room.

"Mrs. McNeill, your husband has sciatica," said the good doctor as though he had just discovered the cure for cancer. "I am going to prescribe a regimen of cortisone shots, that he must have every day for ten days. Now it will hurt him a little temporarily, but the pain should ease up in a few days."

He then sent a nurse to administer the shot with a NEEDLE THAT LONG. My eyes bugged out, and for twenty minutes after that shot (and guess where she stuck that needle!) all I could do was sit and let the tears flow. I never had anything that hurt me so badly in all my life. And I had another nine days to go. Oh! God the pain, and they say men don't cry–baloney!

Georges said he would come visit us on our boat. Only about one out of a hundred that say such things, ever do. Saturday morning, I heard a voice on shore yelling "Fronk". Frank became "Fronk" to Georges and his family. I rowed the dinghy to bring him aboard. He had another bottle of wine and Camembert cheese for us. Specifically he came to invite us to dinner on Sunday. It took no coaxing for us to say yes.

On Sunday Georges and his six year old daughter came to pick us up and take us to his beautiful home a few miles away. Georges was quite a chef as well as an officer in the French Navy and we learned later he did a great many things that took unusual skills. A great guy to have around.

After a magnificent luncheon he said, "Would you like to go swimming? We go every Sunday to a safe beach where the kids can swim and we don't have to worry about currents." My left hip was still hurting so bad from sciatica that I had a terrible limp. We told Georges we would go with him and watch, but not to swim. And watch we did, with out eyes bugged out, for Georges neglected to tell us it was a nude beach. Georges and his family all had swimming gear on. However, we were introduced to many of his friends who didn't wear anything. After they all left and we were sitting in a state of shock, Janet said, "Frank, where in the hell does one look?"

I replied, "You look them straight in the teats."

Janet said, "But mine didn't have teats."

With a grin I quipped, "Then you peeked, shame on you."

Sometimes I think we Americans are so puritanical about nudity it is ridiculous. The French, as well as many other foreign countries, take nudity in their stride and think nothing of it. Nudity just allows them a little more freedom.

Oh, yes, that nice Georges and his family became our very good friends and we shared so many grand experiences with them. Georges was the only one in his family who could speak English, and not much at that. However, we communicated quite well, thank you, by using the French-English translation book and sign language.

We cleared in with the authorities and paid our required bond (since we came down from Hawaii we were required to pay $500.00 each, which was the price of an airline ticket from Tahiti to Hawaii). On leaving Tahiti we would get the bond of $500.00 back without any interest.

We were to move over to Temple Pao Fai beach. The move was to be at slack tide which fell at 6:00 A.M. Janet was at the wheel and had the engine running. I was at the bow, still in agony, trying to raise the anchor. We were both busy and didn't notice the small outrigger canoe that came alongside.

Then a young man tied up the outrigger and climbed aboard the Isle of Barra. He was a policeman who had watched me limp into the Harbor Police office the day before. "Your husband shouldn't be doing this," he said to Janet as he pointed to me laboring on the bow. He walked forward to the bow and ordered me to go back to the cockpit and he proceeded to raise the anchor himself. Then he stayed aboard with us until we were safely anchored at Temple Pao Fai Beach. He did all this on his own time and without being ordered or asked to help. A very nice gesture by a member of Tahitian officialdom. We found all the Tahiti officials very courteous, kind, and helpful.

We moored Tahiti style (two bow anchors out in a `Y' shape and two stern lines tied to bollards on the shore) between two other American boats. It was a great location and the camaraderie among all the sail boats, was wonderful.

Shortly after we arrived we were warned of a gale that would be in our area within a very short time–like about fifteen minutes. We made a check on our anchor and stern lines to make sure they were secure. Other than that there wasn't much to do except secure any loose items on deck.

The gale hit with a vengeance, if you can equivocate a gale to a human thinking person. Next to us was a sailboat thirty two feet long that was blown on the beach. Within minutes a least thirty yachties were on the beach trying to push it back into deep water. I doff my hat to several single handed sailors, who came from out of nowhere to help. They seemed to have more expertise than the regular sailors. They were instrumental in getting a line fastened to the halyard at the top of the mast, then swimming to my boat in very turbulent water with the loose end, had me wrap it around a winch then climbed aboard and helped me winch in until the little boat heeled almost on it's side, freeing the keel from the sandy beach, thence was floated back to deep water. All the single handers scattered as soon as things became normal. They were quite a strange bunch but very dependable in an emergency.

Our first Christmas was spent right there. Of course we would liked to have been home spending this day with our family, but we were dedicated to our dream, so we made the most of it right there. All the yachties got together and celebrated by having a pot luck and exchange of white elephant gifts. A real fun time for all. At midnight an anonymous business man sent several cases of good French champagne to the party. Every

Christmas carol we ever heard and several we hadn't were sung that night. This was an international party made up of people from all around the world. There were about 40 or 50 people still caroling when we reluctantly left the party at three in the morning. We began experiencing a lot of marine growth on the bottom of our boat and thought it high time to haul the boat out and scrape, sand, and prepare the bottom for repainting. We were scheduled to be hauled out and except for starting our engine we were prepared for the next morning haul out at eight o'clock.

About four in the afternoon a French sailboat came into the harbor and dropped his anchor, I would swear right on top of my starboard anchor. I discussed his anchoring with Janet and she said that I better go over and explain that we had to move tomorrow, but it may be very difficult when his boat was atop of our anchor. I took pad and pencil and my French/English dictionary and went over to his boat in our dinghy. Of course he could not speak any English. With sign language, drawings and my poor French I finally got it across to him what I wanted.

He said, "No problem, No problem at all," (or words to that effect). "I leeve et sex tomoro mornin." Great, fine, thank you very much, bid him adieux and left.

Sure enough at six o'clock the next morning he was wearing his business suit, carrying his brief case, got in his dinghy and left for shore not to return. Janet and I stood there dumbfounded. Yeah! No problem for him at all. I told Janet, "To make it on schedule we better start right now." I felt we may have a problem.

We first loosened our stern lines, then took in our port forward anchor. As we began to take in our starboard anchor we came closer and closer to the French boat. A couple of very startled women aboard were wide eyed and perhaps in fear, but I didn't care. The Frenchman was forewarned and didn't seem to give a damn. I took our boat hook and began pushing them away as I continued to haul in my chain. Finally, just at the crucial moment when the French boat would go no further, my anchor came up. It wasn't so bad after all. But, always in the future when

I hear the words, "No Problem," especially from a Frenchman, I cringe, and think, "There just may be a problem."

We hauled out and repainted the bottom of the boat with the aid of our French friends, Georges and his sons. Georges did some necessary welding and other repair work. Georges would have made a great crewman.

After the haul out, we motored inside the reef and entered the small harbor at Maeva Beach. We picked up the mooring buoy closest to the jetty and spent six delightful months there.

Because we paid about $45.00 per month to the Maeva Beach Hotel for our mooring, we had all the privileges of the swimming pool, laundry facilities, ice, and the restaurants. Being male, I watched certain things...like topless women in the swimming pool. You could always tell a topless American women, as she had her arms crossed over her breasts. When she wanted to go in, she would stand on the edge of the pool, uncross her arms and dive in. Well...

The anchorage at Maeva Beach was most pleasant. There was no noise as there was in Papeete on the quay and everything was so convenient. You tied your dinghy to the long jetty and then walked to the street through the hotel grounds. Right out there you could catch a Les Truck to go into town or around the island. A nice arrangement.

Georges and his family, wife Nicole, two sons, Bertram 14 and Fabris 10 and daughter Vamity age six going on sixteen (she was so spoiled I loved every inch of her) came down to the boat often. We would take them out to the hotel's pontoon out by the reef to swim and collect shells. Vamity was a delight. "Plungee," she would yell as she made a run and jumped off the pontoon, holding her nose closed with thumb and forefinger.

Bertram would ride his motor scooter down and I showed him how to work the outboard. He was off by himself for a couple of hours before he returned to the boat hungry as a bear.

Fabris thought it would be a great idea to sleep in our double berth in the fore peak for a night. With his parents' permission all was arranged. I think he was a little homesick but he never said anything and the next day I took him fishing on the reef. The whole family was delightful and we enjoyed them so very much.

Skin diving in the pontoon area was a pure delight. The water was crystal clear and snapping ones fingers underwater would bring up hundreds of beautifully colored tropical fish. There were white tipped sharks further out on the reef but they seemed to be afraid of mankind, so we felt very safe and sheltered. Personally I never saw one, but others had seen a few.

There was the usual gathering of boats from all over the world; America, Australia, Canada, Germany, South Africa and Japan. The whole group of crews gathered often for barbecues on the motu, a small island close by offshore, and one evening was especially memorable. After eating our dinner, some three young men, Tahitians, came through the palm trees carrying guitars and ukeleles. For several hours they entertained us with Tahitian music that raised goose-bumps. They were wonderful.

Usually several members of various boats would get together and team up to play the (new to us) game of "Trivial Pursuit." We borrowed it from the Canadian boat that belonged to one of the three crew members. He complained, "My Trivial Pursuit game, has been invited to more parties than I have."

Janet was the usual winner with her partner, a doctor, who would say, "Let me have all the science questions, Janet, because I'm scientific." All his answers were wrong.

Frankly, all of Tahiti was wonderful. It's a beautiful island and several times we rented cars and drove around it, stopping at many tourist attractions. And, before leaving, we'd always stop at the open market in the center of town. There we'd pick up something for a picnic lunch. The roasted duck and sauce prepared by the Chinese was delicious. That, some French bread (a baguette), a bottle of wine and fresh mangoes and papayas were all you needed.

Nicole introduced us to her brother and his wife (a beautiful Chinese lady. We enjoyed their company and went to many beach parties and their home. The Chinese lady invited us to their home for dinner one night. "I will cook an authentic Chinese dinner for you, you like to eat Chinese style don't you?"

"Oh yes! we said. We often eat Chinese food at home."

"Good! I will kill a dog for you." she said. Then she laughed at our surprised look. "No I wouldn't do that to you, I haven't eaten dog since I was a very young child."

Before we left we were visited by twelve of our friends from various parts of America. One, who is a member of our yacht club in San Diego, swam out to our boat. He said, "I thought you were kidding about sailing around the world and that you had gone to Avalon in Catalina to hide out." Others came, stayed at the Maeva hotel and wined and dined us in tropical splendor. The entertainers got a couple of us out on the dance floor to make perfect asses of ourselves. So what else is new?

It was so difficult to leave Tahiti. We had made so many friends and truly loved the place, but time marches on. So we sailed out of Papeete and crossed the eighteen mile channel to Moorea.

This island is almost impossible to describe. To begin with, it's the most beautiful island on earth. It's peaks, foliage, coves and bays are awe inspiring. We rented a small car and drove around the island and up to the top of the Belvedere, a lookout point. From there we gazed down on Cook's Bay, to see our boat where we were anchored, and could see Pig Bay on the other side. We could also see the many small coves inside the reef. It was all so lovely, and our week there was sheer pleasure. Every evening was perfect, but one evening was especially so. In fact, I let out a big sigh.

Janet turned to me and said, "Frank is there something wrong?"

"Oh no!" I said, "Everything is just right. Look around you. What do you see and smell?"

She replied, "I see and smell a lot of things, what's with you?"

"Well I see a beautiful tropical island, with tall palm tree swaying in the breeze. There are no conventional type buildings and none higher than a palm tree, all thatched and native style and with their own generators for electricity. And I see Les Trucks going by full of natives and they are singing their native songs, and I smell the pineapple field wafting the aroma of pineapple all around this area, plus all the smells of the plumaria and other flowers from the island."

Whereupon Janet let out a big sigh an said, "Oh Wow! I could get so used to this."

So could I...So could I.

One memorable experience was watching *Wanderer V* sail in as the weather kicked up. *Wanderer V* was owned by Susan and Eric Hiscock. Eric was one of the most prolific writers of books about sailors and sailing in modern times. He was so positive in his writings and always made you feel good. So we shared Cook's Bay for four days with Susan and Eric Hiscock. Badly we wanted to rap on his hull and say "Mr. Hiscock we've bought and read everything you've ever written and we think you're wonderful!" But we'd heard that he valued his privacy, so we didn't disturb him.

We left Cook's Bay late one afternoon (the channel out through the reef is glorious) for the overnight sail to Huahine. Then the weather closed in and the rains came. With clouds so low that we couldn't see anything, much less the island we were heading for, we depended solely on our SATNAV to keep us on the right path. Unfortunately we were not getting hourly fixes on our SATNAV in the southern hemisphere. It was more like ten to thirteen hours between fixes. Our latest fix had been several hours old when we were trying to find the channel to go into Huahine.

Finally, after much sailing back and forth looking for the channel and one near miss, we found the opening in the reef. The near miss occurred as we were looking for the markers on either side of the reef pass. I was on the bow trying to peer through the haze when I shouted, "There they are!" There indeed were the two black markers in view and Janet sailed toward them. Suddenly one marker bent over. I almost froze, but yelled, "Hard alee!" and Janet really spun the wheel over. The two "markers" were fishermen standing on the reef. Fortunately one of them dropped something or we'd have carved a new opening through the reef.

21

We moved north and found the reef pass when another boat came through it. We followed the channel in and anchored in the small bay off the village of Fare. There we refueled and topped off our water tanks. The latter was a mistake. Due to the heavy rains the Huahine water supply had become contaminated and Janet paid for it later. I had strained the water carefully and added chlorine, but it wasn't enough.

It was at Huahine that we met Doug and Dolores. Doug was an excellent bridge player. Dolores was just a beginner. They were newlyweds and were very much in love. We didn't get to know them very well then, but they became very close friends much later.

I was very concerned about the safety of the small overcrowded anchorage at Fare so we stayed just two days and then left for Raiatea. That island was just a few miles away and the pass through the reef was clearly marked so there was no problem. We anchored off the village and checked in with the authorities. Then we motored inside the reef to the marina at Apooiti. It is on the north west corner of the island and is small but secure. We pulled into a slip and tied up. Then the bad water from Huahine struck.

Janet became ill and had to see a doctor. A friend from the marina, one fluent in French, took her to the hospital. There she was examined, given an injection with a needle THAT long and two prescriptions which the doctor filled himself. The total charge for all this treatment was $1.20 US. Medicine in French Polynesia is socialistic and very competent.

Janet recovered after five days on a strict diet of plain boiled rice for every meal. Yeck! But if you are ill, boiled rice has a way of curing you. During the interim we made plans for leaving Raiatea. We wanted to be on Bora Bora for the Fete.

What is the Fete? That's the 14th of July, Bastille day, and a national holiday. It lasts just one day in France and one month in French Polynesia. And we had been told it was a wonderful celebration to see.

The reef that surrounds Raiatea also surrounds the island of Ta'haa. Another beautiful island to see, but we had no intentions of stopping there. They've made it difficult to check in there for the necessary village is WAY over on the other side. As we motored past we could see many beautiful coves and one very large bay that was tempting. However, we raised the sails and went on past and through the pass in the reef. The swells in the ocean were monstrous, but flattened out as we neared Bora Bora.

There is but one opening in the reef at Bora Bora, far over on the western side. We sailed through it and went up to the anchorage in front of the Hotel Oa Oa where we saw a wonderful sign, "SAILBOATS WELCOME". We understand that the Hotel Oa Oa is no longer there, and that's a shame, for it was a welcome haven for sail boats. At the time we sailed in, a man on the dock motioned us to the last mooring buoy available. We picked it up and tied firmly to the buoy. The mooring buoys were a blessing for the bay at Bora Bora is about 90 feet deep. And the holding is iffy at best.

Bora Bora, while not as beautiful as Moorea, was charming. We rented bicycles and rode around the island. We stopped at Bloody Mary's Hotel on the southwest corner of the island and had a delightful lunch prepared by the owner. This hotel is a hangout for the great and near great, the food was excellent and the ambience most delightful. And there's one striking element about this hotel. You've heard a toilet called a "throne" haven't you? Well, at Bloody Mary's it is a reality. Located in the center of the dining room, it is surrounded by a fence of stakes about five feet high. The toilet is on a raised platform and when you're seated on it you can look all over the whole room. And all the people can look back at you. If you demand privacy on such occasions then it isn't for you.

Shortly after we arrived, Doug and Dolores came in. We became constant companions, riding bikes, sightseeing and doing all the tourist's things, and in our spare time we taught Dolores how to play bridge. She caught on very fast and before long she was playing very well for an amateur. We had many sessions of bridge, but really enjoyed each others company. We love bridge but when it gets in the way of our conversation, the heck with bridge.

One evening we were on their boat playing bridge. Dolores said, "Doesn't anyone feel the boat rocking, I don't feel so good," and she looked a little green around the gills.

Immediately Doug said, "Dolores, you don't have your wristband on, I'll get it for you." After he placed it on her wrist for about five minutes color came back in her cheeks and she said, "Deal the cards."

"Whoa!" Janet said, "what is this band?" We had never heard of it.

"It's a pressure sensitive band and wearing it properly, one should never be sea, air, or carsick. You can get them at most chandleries and probably large sporting good stores." said Doug.

After examining the wristband, Janet said, "They are very simple, I could make them." In the next week she made a dozen of them. They don't work for everybody, but I wouldn't be without mine. Yes even though I have sailed 54,000 miles in my boat and probably three or four times that on U.S. Navy boats, I get a little queasy when going out to sea after about six months in port and with my wristband it helps me get my sea legs a lot quicker.

As advertised, the Fete was a must see. It lived up to its reputation, and we found it impossible to stay away. A French naval vessel came in and tied to the village dock. Decorated with brightly colored flags it lent a festive touch to the bay. Little shops and restaurants, covered with coconut palm fronds, were set up all along the dock and around the square. They served delicious food and we took advantage of that.

Then came the great celebration of the Fete. All of the small villages on the island competed against each other. Every citizen in those villages, from the oldest to the youngest, took part in the singing and dancing. Wearing costumes made of identical material and competing between villages with different designs that they had made themselves, they presented a colorful picture. The singing and dancing was marvelous and the drum beats contagious. Previously, while listening to all the drumming being rehearsed, Janet would remark, "Well, they're boiling another missionary." Instead they were beating out the fantastic rhythms to which the dancers performed. The Fete on Bora Bora is not to be missed.

As we were leaving Bora Bora, Doug and Dolores were right behind us coming out the channel. Janet and Doug were on the VHF talking with each other and saying goodbye. We were still headed in a westerly direction to attain our goal we had set. Doug and Dolores were headed back to San Francisco via Hawaii. Being with them almost constantly for about a month, it was a poignant scene as each became more blubbery in saying goodbye. If anyone had heard that conversation, I'm sure they would have said, "My God! Is this the end, I wonder who died?" It would be many years before we would get together again.

When leaving Bora Bora, we intended to stop at the smaller Polynesian islands of Maupiti and Mopelia. With only one small opening in each of their reefs those stops were impossible. Heavy seas were breaking over the openings and even a large ferry was stopped. So instead we thought we'd go north to Suvarov Island which is part of the Cook Islands that belong to New Zealand. But on the HAM radio we heard all of the boats in that small anchorage saying that they were standing 24 hour anchor watches as the surf was coming over the reef. We decided we didn't need that so we turned west for American Samoa.

When we left Bora Bora we found that we couldn't look back. The South Pacific is indeed paradise and French Polynesia is its epitome.

CHAPTER TWO

The passage from Bora Bora to American Samoa was a bear. Only 1200 miles, and our shortest passage yet. But the weather never let up. There wasn't one single day we could say we had salubrious sailing. There was rain, squalls that came up at a moment's notice, and freaky winds. One day the wind changed direction about every 15 minutes. At almost any given time we would be on a port tack. In another 15 minutes time we would be on a starboard tack. The wind was changing repeatedly. I nearly went crazy changing the sails, coming about and then gibing. Finally, in a fit of despair, I said to Janet, "I'm pulling down the sails until the winds settles and ends this silliness."

And finally it did, about three hours later. In the meantime we just sat and bobbed. Every day the wind had it's spell of trying to make me crazy. I would say to Janet, "Honey, the wind has got to change and maybe tomorrow will be better."

The big island of Tutuila was a most welcome sight. The entrance into the big L-shaped bay was clearly marked and if you follow all the buoys there is no problem. And we had none. None, that is, until we contacted the authorities from our tie-up on the jetty. They informed us that their office was closed and if they came down to the boat we would have to pay them $10.00 an hour each. I asked how many there would be and how long it would take. The answer was four persons and it might take two hours. I asked what the fee was during regular working hours and was told it was a free inspection. I am neither stupid or rich so told them to wait until morning to clear us in.

The officer told us that we would have to leave the harbor and go out to sea again. At this remark I almost lost my cool. I told him that there was a gale out there and that we had been in terrible weather for ten days and we weren't going anywhere. Also that we were terribly tired and needed a rest. The officer said, "Oh! I didn't know that," and told me to tie up to a boat at the dock and they'd clear us in the next morning. But we did break their rule. We weren't supposed to leave our boat. When we sailed in we saw a boat that had been our neighbor at Temple Pao Fai Beach in Papeete. They called us on the VHF with an invitation to dinner. So we dinghied over and had a lovely evening. The captain of that boat had a weather fax and he said, "You guys had a miserable trip, didn't you?" We answered him affirmatively and asked how he knew. He laughed and showed us the printout from his new weather fax he had recently purchased. It said that we'd gone through two tropical depressions and one tropical convergence zone. We told him that we knew they were nasty, we just didn't know that they had names.

The next morning only one official came down to the dock. He shouted to us and I had to take my ships papers to him on the dock. The check in ceremony was very brief and informal. The official asked if we had weapons aboard. I told him we did, told him what kind and with so much ammunition. The official said, "Well try not to shoot anybody while you are here." That was almost prophetic. as it was a great temptation for us to do just that. Well, so much for the officials at $10.00 an hour each for overtime.

The main reason we went into Pago Pago was so we could fly Space A (availability of seats on a U.S. military aircraft). The planes land at Pago Pago and we intended to catch one of them. Janet's mother had been very ill and we felt compelled to visit her. But first we had to find a boat sitter for our absence.

The boat we were first tied to at the jetty was a missionary boat and the Captain of that vessel recommended a man he said was reliable. We met him and contracted with him to watch our boat for three months while we were gone, paying him the first month fee in advance. Then we caught the next plane that would take us to California.

When we returned in three months we were horrified. I

opened the main hatch and let out an exclamation not to be heard by delicate ears. I didn't want Janet to see, but knew that she had to. The whole interior was moving–cockroaches–everywhere. Our reliable boat sitter had moved aboard the boat with his girlfriend, which he wasn't supposed to do, and in all the time we were gone he (they) hadn't washed a dish, pan, sheet, towel or cleaned the toilet. As if that weren't enough he had left every port and hatch open and it rains about 300 inches a year in Samoa. Everything was soaked.

I dashed out and bought a whole bunch of bug bombs and, after we gathered up the laundry, set them off in several places, closed up, and left the boat. It took us six hours to do the laundry at the laundromat WAY out toward the west end of the island. We rented a car for a few days until we could get the mess cleaned and things returned to normal. When we returned to the boat it was full of dead cockroaches. With a shovel we scooped them into a five gallon bucket and dumped them. Another bucket later all the little bodies were gone. But we knew we didn't kill all of them. We bombed them several times at regular intervals and used several pounds of boric acid. On the third bombing we only got a smattering of the weird looking creatures. It wasn't until four years later that we finally got rid of them. They were certainly prolific. I now understand how cockroaches have survived for millions of years.

Then we had to take care of all the wet cushions and mattresses in the boat. We had planned to go on to Fiji, but decided to stop spinning our wheels and get the boat back to Bristol fashion first. And that decision probably saved our lives. Fiji was hit with three typhoons one right after another and all the boats in the harbor were sent onto the rocks and many people drowned. So we have something to thank American Samoa for. Ye Gods! not cockroaches.

On returning from San Diego and clearing in with the harbor master, we had moved our boat over to the lagoon behind the jetty and among the other cruisers. Some of them had been there for years as they had good jobs on the island. American Samoa is one of the few places where you are permitted to work and if you have any talent at all you can find a job. Also there isn't much to do in Pago Pago. So a job is the only answer.

We knew we would be in Pago Pago for quite a long time, therefore a job was really needed to while away the time. However, the boat needed many hours of maintenance and TLC. I felt that I could not spare the time away from the boat. Anyway I was retired and couldn't see going back to an eight to five routine. Janet would only be a hindrance to a lot of my work, so I told her if she wanted to work, to see if she could get a job as a reporter or something on the newspaper. The *Samoan Journal* was advertising for help.

The interview Janet had at the *Samoan Journal* was the least difficult job she had ever applied for. Janet walked into Rowena's office (the publisher) and said, "My name is Janet McNeill and....."

"Good, you're hired, your desk is right over there. You will be chief editor of the English section and you will be paid xxx dollars a month. Do you have any questions?"

After such a blunt, direct employment, Janet wasn't about to open her big mouth and spoil things. She sat down at the electric IBM typewriter and began an editorial for the next issue. She wrote, "My name is Janet McNeill and I have just been hired as your editor of the English section of this newspaper. While I am here..." She finished her piece and sent a note to me she had got the job and wouldn't be home to dinner until about 5:00 P.M.

Janet was not only the editor, but also reporter for many articles as well. About six weeks later a guy came in and wanted to speak to the sports reporter. Janet was up to her eyebrows in work and was shaking her head "NO" at Rowena. Rowena said, "I'm sorry but our sports writer is doing an interview over on Western Samoa and he will be gone until Friday. Can I help you?"

The man said, "I have been reading this paper for years. I read it because it has only been slightly better than your competitor. Lately, there has been a big improvement in the paper as a whole, and without a subscription, you can't find one anywhere. The *Journal* now is the best I've ever read. Its newsy, historical and full of warm human interest stories. I just wanted to compliment the sports writer for writing such fine articles."

Rowena thanked the man for all his compliments, then said, "as soon as our sports writer returns, I will give him the message."

After the man left, Rowena turned to Janet and said "Janet you have just earned yourself a raise, but how do you write those articles with such verve?"

Janet replied, "Well, you know all those two or three sentence Associated Press news release clippings we get. I take them and embellish them a little from what my father taught me. When I was very young my father took me to every sports game that we could possibly see–football, basketball, baseball, soccer, tennis, volleyball etc. My father was a sports nut and that is about all he talked about. He knew the names of all the major league teams, their averages, handicaps, whatever. Some of the stories, I remember and just write them that way. My father would have been a great sports writer."

Janet came home one night visibly shaken and threw her purse on the settee. Our little twenty-five automatic fell out. I looked at it for a moment, then looked at her and said, "Janet I want to know and I want to know right now," pointing to the little weapon, "WHAT ARE YOU DOING WITH THIS–WHAT THE HELL IS GOING ON?"

"Not now, let me eat first before I fall on my face. Then I'll tell you."

Living with Janet with her diabetic condition for many years, I knew it would rile her and make the situation worse if I pushed her.

"Fair enough," I said, and we sat down to dinner with a little wine to calm both of us a little. After dinner and the dishes were done, Janet told me this unbelievable story.

The governor (newly elected) had appointed a man to the second most powerful position on the Island. His job was commissioner of public safety. He was in charge of the police force, fire fighters, health, you name it. This man had a police record longer than your arm. He had been arrested many times for things such as drunk and disorderly, DUI, child molesting, wife beating, etc. He had been acquitted on three separate murder charges.

Janet had tried many times to reach the governor for an interview to question him on the reasons he had appointed such a man in this position of responsibility and authority. The governor would not comply with Janet's request to return her telephone calls or give her an interview. So eventually, she wrote articles, "Where is the body buried Governor?" "What does this man have on you, Governor, that you place him in such a position, etc?" She began to publish all the public records of the commissioner's weird behavior. Rowena had previously told Janet that she could print anything in the paper as long as it was the truth.

Word spread that this commissioner was about to erase this little pest of an editor, and it was known by some police officials that he was going to eliminate the nuisance. Because of this threat, the commissioner's own police force had him followed everywhere he went and sent a patrol car to patrol the dock area where our boat was tied and the area where Janet worked. A high ranking police official and a good friend told Janet, "Oh! we will not let him get close to you to do you harm. However, there is the possibility that he will hire someone to do you in. We do our best, but there is little protection we can give you for that."

I then told Janet, "If you shot that bastard with this little twenty-five automatic, you would only make him mad, as it would only feel like a bee sting to him. You would only aggravate him. You know he is a big as a barn door. Therefore, in the future you will take our "Police Positive Thirty-Eight," or I will escort you to and from work. From that day on the big pistol was in my hand with the safety off inside a paper bag. When we arrived at her office the pistol was transferred to a handy place in her desk. I would also escort Janet back to the boat each evening.

Our yachting neighbors became aware of how often the police cars were patrolling the area. Then finally they figured out that it must be our boat that they were watching, observing, and protecting and asked us, "What's going on?" When they found out the real purpose, they were very apprehensive. Our next door neighbor said, "Thank God we have a steel hull boat." Some of our neighbors knew that we would leave Pago Pago, and could hardly wait until we did.

Rowena answered the telephone one day while I was there at the newspaper office. She said, "What? What did you say?" There was a short pause, then she said, "Well sir, if you are going to firebomb us, you will have to come down here to the newspaper, you can't do it over the telephone." Then she replaced the telephone in its cradle. I ask her if she got many calls like that and how it made her feel. She told me that at first it was a very disconcerting, but after several such calls, she labeled them as idle threats. From that moment on, for sanity's sake, I banked on it as being an idle threat. However, I could not have lived with myself if something had happened to Janet. I was apprehensive and never took a thing for granted and watched her like a hawk, although she never knew it. As far as I know the *Samoa Journal* is still in operation and nothing has happened.

After a time with no response from the governor, Janet made copies of all court records, police records, and the appointment of this man to high office. Janet mailed a copy to the Secretary of Interior of the United States, and to the Democratic Senators of California and Hawaii with cover letters stating that she thought the U. S. Government should know what the tax payers of America were getting for their money.

We found out much later that six weeks after we left American Samoa, the Secretary of Interior of the United States had made a surprise visit to American Samoa and two days after his inspection, the rotten commissioner was out of office. Rowena's husband Jake called us by telephone and said, "Janet, you dug deep and you dug dirty, but you got rid of that son of a bitch. We from the *Journal* and the people of American Samoa want to thank you and to let you know we really appreciate all your efforts."

Janet said, "If I come back will I get my old job back?" He

told her to get back as fast as possible with double her salary. It seems a crying shame that more dirty rotten politicians are in office and not much is being done to oust them.

American Samoa is probably the best natural harbor in the middle of the Pacific, but it's not a very nice place. The American tuna fleet has moved there and the bay is filthy. The tuna clippers wash out their storage compartments and the bay is full of blood and so polluted. Everyone that tries to swim in the bay, even the area where it looks clean sometimes, develops a horrible rash all over their body. And the smells from the tuna canneries drains all your sinus cavities. It's horrible. And with all that blood in the water it attracts the sharks. So that rules out sailing, surfing, and water skiing.

Tutuila is really beautiful, but it's awfully dirty. And the local government is the most corrupt organization we have ever seen. But we understood from cruisers that had visited other island groups that all of them lack honesty. It's such a shame for the islands. The people deserve better than that. We were in American Samoa in 1983-1984 (about eleven months), but we have read that it hasn't improved any. And that's too bad.

Janet loved her job at the *Samoa Journal* and *Advertiser* during our stay there. She was given a great insight into the internal workings of the island and most of it was terribly depressing and discouraging. However, we knew we wouldn't be there forever, but the poor Samoans were stuck with it.

While Janet was at her job as editor, I played boat wife, doing the cooking, laundry, provisioning, and working on a very cranky engine and trying to learn the French language by cassette tapes. Janet always seemed quite amazed at my talents. Maybe that is why we got along so well. One day Janet had the company car and was going to interview some people. She asked if I wanted to go along. Sure, why not. It was close to four o'clock when Janet was through interviewing. On the way back she asked me to go on to the office with her, she would have about fifteen minutes work and then we could walk home together. I objected very strenuously and said, "Oh no if I don't get back to the boat right away and get my potatoes in and the meat loaf started we won't get to eat until ten o'clock."

Janet burst out laughing and said, "I've been doing that to you for years and now you are getting even."

One of the blessings of American Samoa is that all American food products are available. While we loved the French food in French Polynesia, it was great to get back to good old American treats. And another real treat in Pago Pago was the tuna available and because of that Pago Pago is known as the "Sashimi Capital" of the world. Sashimi is raw tuna, sliced very thin and dipped into a hot oriental mustard mixed with soy sauce. One day I bought a whole tuna and we ate it, the whole thing, that same day, dipped in the marinade sauce as required. What a feast.

Because of Janet's job we were invited to many activities on the island. And we made many friends among the Samoan people. One high chief invited us to his village on the north side of the island. It was in a picture-postcard setting with a snow white sandy beach running for about a mile and a half. Lined with graceful palm trees and seen against a clear blue sky and surf, it was breathtaking. Only people with the chief's permission were allowed on the beach. We were enjoying a beach site that dozens of tourists down the way would have given their eyeteeth to have used.

Another high chief invited us to his home up in the Pago Pago Valley for a family party. They roasted a whole pig that was served with coconut cream wrapped in taro leaves and roasted with the pig. It was a fantastic meal. Non-fattening of course!

And when it was time for us to leave we were given several farewell parties. One was hosted by a high chief and his wife and was at his home on the east end of the island. He had invited mostly non-Samoans as guests and it was a wonderful relaxed evening. I believe that most of the people were very appreciative of Janet's work as editor on the *Journal* and giving us a party was a way to say thank you.

Then the staff of the newspaper gave another party at the hotel. Janet had enjoyed her association with them and there wasn't a dry eye to be seen when we said our goodbyes.

Our passage to Fiji was very slow. The winds were nonexistent. When albatross sit on your bow pulpit and fall asleep, you know you're going slowly. And we were taking the long way around in order to avoid the Lau Group of atolls and reefs. About a dozen boats each year are lost on those reefs and we wanted no part of them. So we went north of the Fijian Islands which added about 200 miles to a 1200 mile passage. But there was much less turmoil and worry. We had friends who lost their boat in the Lau Group and were on the reef for 36 hours before they were rescued. Other friends said that the Lau Group terrified them and it was the only time they thought they would lose their boat. So, no thank you.

On this passage the epitome of "Murphy's Law" was all too repetitious. What could go wrong, did, and sometimes repeatedly. I had air-freighted (at great expense) from Hawaii to American Samoa some coolant system parts for the main engine. They were not the correct size, but the only parts available and they did work for a short time before the engine heated up and then would have to be shut down.

The engine had to be shut off to cool for a couple hours for a run of only about ten minutes of operation. I had to repair or replace bilge pumps, water pumps, a broken shroud, several frayed sheets (sail lines) and halyards, plus many electrical or electronic parts or wiring that had stopped because of corrosion. There was no stopping of the difficulties. Janet had an infection and fever. I put her on antibiotics and to bed for a few days and carried on her duties. I myself had an infection on my left thumb that was very painful and was very awkward when I had to repair a bilge pump or do some other duties requiring both hands. Boating really becomes paradigmatic when Murphy's law sets in. Oh! Boy!

When we made the turn around the southwestern corner of Viti Levu and into the Kandavu Pass the wind and currents were against us. It was very difficult to make any forward movement. But we did, thanks to a Japanese freighter, the *Shinkai Maru,* who reluctantly towed us into Suva. The towing had slowed their progress by several hours. I went over to the main dock the next day with a bottle of Scotch for the Japanese Captain, but the *Shinkai Maru* had already left. So a belated thank you, Captain.

Suva was a pleasant anchorage. Just off the Royal Suva Yacht Club the bottom was soft mud and the holding iffy. But the yacht club was a delight. The personnel and members were so friendly and hospitable and their dining room served delicious food. Everywhere we have gone we have eaten the food that the natives eat. It has always been tasty and pleasant and, in many cases, a delightful surprise. The open market in Suva was terrific. So many fresh fruits and vegetables and the meat market across the street was very reasonable. We pigged out on their racks of lamb. Tender and tasty.

While we were still in Suva a large group of boats sailed in. They were entered in the Auckland, New Zealand to Suva Race and were resting up before beginning the return sail. A small craft weather warning was in process for the Kandavu Passage so all of the racing boats and the cruising boats that wanted to leave had to postpone their departure. Four days later the weather warning was lifted so eleven boats went out through the reef pass and down the Kandavu Passage.

CHAPTER THREE

When any boat leaves Suva they must file a sail plan. Similar to an airplane's flight plan, it lists your destination, all the particulars of your boat and your next of kin. The Tasman Sea has a horrible reputation as being a wide stretch of very rough water cursed with storms. Then, on the other hand, it can be a milk run as we have friends who have crossed it three times and had to motor the whole way–no wind at all. But that wasn't to be our case. The day we tried the milk curdled.

We had planned on an 11 to 12 day passage to Coff's Harbor, Australia, but Janet had stocked food for double that time and then added enough for an extra 12 days. And it's a good thing she did. All that food and the extras from American Samoa kept us going. For our 11-12 day passage took 49 days.

The first day out of Suva was wonderful. The skies were clear and blue and the seas were smooth. We averaged seven knots as we headed out of the Kandavu Passage. We were the only boat heading southwest to Australia, as all the others were going either to New Zealand or southeast to Tonga. We had a salubrious sale that first day making 149 miles.

The next morning the skies were overcast and the wind and seas had both picked up a little. But Suva Radio was saying "10 to 12 knot winds and moderate seas," so we felt no apprehensions. The next day the wind really picked up to gale force (35 to 40 knots) and the seas were becoming quite rough. The waves were 15 to 20 feet tall and were breaking over the bow.

I went up on the bow and put up the storm sails and that whole procedure scared Janet about half to death. When the waves would break she couldn't see me, then the water would run off of me and spill over the side of the boat and she could see my orange life jacket again. Each time that happened I think she died just a little. It wasn't much fun getting thoroughly drenched either. When the storm sails were finally hanked on and raised I returned to the cockpit, Janet grabbed my jacket and pulled me down inside to safety and was shivering from fright. It was as if I'd been up there for six months. She was trembling. She was happy to have me back in the cockpit. I was also.

The fourth day was even worse. I tried to take some video shots of the waves, but even strapped on with my safety harness, I couldn't hold the camera steady enough. Then on the fifth day all hell broke loose. The winds were 80 to 100 knots and the seas were 35 to 45 feet high or higher. You couldn't see more than a few feet as salt water spray filled the air and foam was blowing thicker than frosting on a Texas chocolate cake. Suva Radio was still saying "10 to 12 knot winds and moderate seas." They were completely out of touch with reality. So we turned on our HAM radio and heard boats in distress all over the southwestern Pacific.

How a storm of such magnitude could go undetected and unpredicted was a puzzle to us. Later, when talking to a retired weatherman, he said that when they see a blob on the radar that is over the Tasman they just assume it's another rotten Tasman day. But they don't know what's underneath that blob. And that time it was in hurricane force winds.

As we were in that necklace of atolls, reefs and small islands that stretch from New Caledonia to Fiji, we didn't dare heave to and stop. We had to get out of there. In fact one SAT-NAV fix showed that we were within about ten feet from shore of a small atoll, but because of waves, spray, and foam we had no visibility further than the life rail. So we ran before the storm for 20 hours, making 9 1/2 knots the whole time with our handkerchief sized storm sails. Between us, it was decided we had enough distance from the hard things that make holes in your hull, so we could stop. We both calculated that for every mile we made forward we were pushed back close to 1/2 mile, but we were now in the open sea.

We set the sails for heaving to and then brought the bow into the wind. Just then a rogue wave slammed into our port side tearing off a shroud in the rigging and breaking a spreader both on the port side of the mast and ripping out our cockpit cover. Thanks to the manufacturers for strong safety harnesses, as we were securely hooked on. Everything that could float was going over the side and we grabbed what we could. Then we dove below and battened down the main hatch.

We have a board set into slides underneath our dinette table so that, when at sea, things stored under there won't slide around. There's room between that board and our settee for cushions on the deck so we put the settee seat and back cushion there. Then we piled pillows all around us, squeezed in and hanged on to each other. We had to shout sweet nothings to each other for you couldn't hear whispered ones.

It was an awful night. We bounced up and down like a cork and it sounded as if freight trains were going across the deck or smashing into the sides of our hull. The sounds were most frightening, with the winds whistling in the rigging, and there was a horrible pounding sound. Janet didn't panic but wanted to be reassured. "Honey are we going to make it?"

With my fingers crossed behind my back, I replied, "Janet we built this boat. You know how strong it is. Sure, we are going to make it." With that reassurance she managed to get a little sleep. I couldn't sleep.

The next morning I had to find out what that pounding sound in the cockpit was so I slid back the main hatch and looked out. I rarely lose my cool and in a very calm voice said, "Janet, you'd better come look. I think we may have a problem."

Janet looked and we did have a problem. The binnacle was laying on its side and all the controls leading to the rudder and the diesel engine were flopping around the cockpit. An angry Pacific Ocean had shown its strength. All of the waves beating into the cockpit had broken the 6 inch long 1/4 inch thick stainless bolts that held the binnacle had snapped off as if they were toothpicks. And that pounding sound we heard was the rudder oscillating about and hitting the hull. Afraid that the rudder movement would, in time, put a hole the hull, I set about making repairs. With the boat pitching wildly, most of the time one was lucky just to hang on; working conditions were almost impossible. I worked feverishly for over four hours, until I got the rudder secured fore and aft using shock cord and 1/4 inch Nylon line. I wasn't sure but thought there may be more damage already done. I found out much later there wasn't enough damage to repair to the underside of the hull so just painted over the area of the hull where the rudder had been pounding. But the movement of the rudder was so strong that I had to replace the restraints about every four hours. Wave action would cause the rudder to oscillate, breaking the restraints I had emplaced.

At one time the fluctuation of the water moved the rudder with great force. My arm was caught between rudder arm and the structure of the boat. It gave me a very nasty bruise which resulted in black and blue spots that lasted for many days. Most fortunate though my arm was not broken. In between times of replacing broken strands of shock cord and Nylon line, we slept.

After 3 1/2 days the winds subsided and the seas calmed a little. We contacted Tony's Net in the southwestern Pacific and told them we had port rigging damage and that we had lost our steering, but we had figured out how to jury-rig a steering system and I set about doing that. Tony's Net control (Don Hopper) asked our intentions, position and damage report. We replied that we had sustained an awfully lot of damage. We felt that by going to Coff's harbor as originally planned that the necessary repair work could not possibly be made. I felt the only large place in Australia that could handle our myriad of problems would be Sydney. And we had that very morning planned a course for Sydney. It never occurred to us that we wouldn't make it.

The very next day I had the steering system going. Using the three foot long fiberglass rudder of our wind vane and securing it with shock cord to blocks and around cleats, we could steer, not well, but satisfactorily under the circumstances. There was no coming about or tacking normally. Because the wind vane rudder was so small we made very large circles so we couldn't bring the bow across the wind; therefore, we had a lot of controlled gibes when we wanted to tack.

Also on this day we discovered that our engine wouldn't start. Only later did we find that salt water had backed up the exhaust and killed it. Then, horror of horrors, the HAM radio went out. We could still receive, but couldn't transmit. The storm had nothing to do with that. It was a manufacturer's defect in the logic board. Swell. That's all we needed. But the HAM Net assumed that we could still hear and continued to broadcast weather reports to us. We were most grateful.

Of the 44 days adrift 34 of them were in absolutely calm water. The calm would come at spaced intervals. The longest period of calm was 16 days, and we were about to go nuts when happily for us a gale came up. We would throw out our trash at night and the next morning it was still floating around us. In fact, were it not for the four gales that came along after the initial storm, we wouldn't have made any forward progress at all.

As our solar panel was functioning and charging our batteries at a minuscule rate our SATNAV kept us up to date on our position. So we were never lost. However, everyone said later, "When you were lost", a statement that rather bugged me. But we thought we would never get around Lord Howe Island. We were at the mercy of the winds, being able to a limited sail only. I had jury-rigged a Dacron line for the broken shroud and we could sail with small sails on the port tack. On a starboard tack, I put up the larger sails. So whichever way the wind blew, that's the way we went. The chart looked as is some drunk was drawing designs on it as we zigzagged all over.

On the 21st day after our last call to the HAM Net, we tuned in for a weather report and heard them talking about us. It was like listening to our own funeral. "Too bad we lost the McNeills. Nice people," and so on. We were shouting, "We're here, We're here. We're not dead." Then we heard them say that they had informed our son (who lived near Melbourne) that we were missing at sea and assumed dead. We just kept our fingers crossed that he would not cash in on the insurance. They also said that the navies and air forces of Australia, New Zealand and New Caledonia (French) were looking for us. That was encouraging.

To draw attention to any passing ship or aircraft about our handicapped boat, Janet sewed all of our red bath towels together and we put them over the top of the cockpit cover. We flew our largest (4' x 6') American flag upside down and raised a Delta flag (I am disabled) and a Foxtrot flag (I am maneuvering with great difficulty, contact me) and felt we were ready for any boat to come along. But none did.

Those many days at sea weren't all terrifying. The calms were rather nerve wracking for we wanted to make some progress. But in the meantime we read books, played games, made fudge, and baked cookies. And one day we even popped some corn. But, to be honest, the days did drag. We had time to design a doll's house for our granddaughter and a model train layout for our grandson. Oh, yes, Janet owes me about $4,000,000 in gin rummy losses. She claims that I cheat.

I tried to catch a mahi mahi that was swimming in a school of over a dozen. All those fish were probably close to seven or eight pounds and would have made for some delicious eating. I couldn't reel in fast enough after casting to lure a fish near the line. No matter what I did, I was skunked on fishing.

Once, west of Lord Howe Island, we did hear two small planes flying over us. The sky was overcast but I thought it worthwhile to fire off two parachute red flares. I was hoping they'd penetrate the cloud cover, but the clouds were too high and the planes flew on. Also, we tried to contact the planes with the VHF and no answer there either. We learned later that the Australian planes did not carry VHF radios.

One windless night we watched as a huge jet airliner flew over us. Flying out of Sydney, it was going east. Janet said,. "Honey, our bow is pointing in the wrong direction."

I replied, "But we're not going anywhere."

Janet gave a couple of sniffles and said, "But we're still pointing the wrong way. What if the wind comes up?"

"Then I'll turn the bow in the other direction." Two more sniffles and I gave in with a sigh of defeat. I grabbed a dinghy oar and spent the next two hours pointing the bow toward the southwest. We still weren't going anywhere, but it was a great morale booster to Janet.

On the 45th day at sea we could see land on the horizon. According to our SATNAV it was Crowdy Head on Australia's southeast coast. We had one small bottle of champagne left so we popped its cork and poured out the two glasses it held. We celebrated our first ocean crossed entirely by our own hands. We toasted the Pacific Ocean, the boat, each other, the President of the United States, the Queen of England and the Prime Minister of Australia. Then we sailed on south.

It was on the 48th day after leaving Suva that we finally saw light at the end of the tunnel. Janet was below doing the breakfast dishes when she saw a huge freighter through the port. The only radio that still operable was a small handheld VHF with penlight batteries. She called and the Norwegian vessel *Kiwi Arrow* answered. They were very suspicious because three weeks before we disappeared a boat had left Coff"s Harbor and hadn't been seen since. Some ghouls on the coast were putting out fake position calls pretending to be the crew of that missing boat. So the rescue forces were going every which way trying to find them. Apparently the word had spread for the *Kiwi Arrow* viewed us with suspicion.

After many questions the *Kiwi Arrow* decided we were telling the truth and said they were coming to tow us to Newcastle. Janet asked how far to Newcastle. "60 nautical miles," was the answer. "How far to Sydney?" she asked. "90 nautical miles," she was told. After they said they were going to tow us to Newcastle, I kept shaking my head no and telling Janet to tell the ship that we would go on to Sydney and to thank the *Kiwi Arrow* for their kind offer of help. The radio operator said that at the rate we were going it would take us about three days. We were apparently going backwards at the time. Then we asked them to notify Sydney Radio and ask if they would notify our son that we were alive and well and on our way south. We had to admit to sinking hearts as the huge ship went out of sight. But we'd sailed over a 1000 miles with terrible steering conditions and we felt we could make that last 90 on our own.

Now when Janet prays she comes right to the point. She

says that when you talk to God don't mumble, speak up. I told Janet that if I prayed the way she does God would strike me dead with a lightning bolt. So I listened fearfully as she began. "God, we need wind. We don't want to go south, east, or north. We want to go southwest on course 230 degrees, not 240 degrees, not 220 degrees, but 230 degrees which would be very nice. Now give us that wind and let's go. Now God get with it!"

Within an hour the wind picked up and soon we were in a full blown gale. Janet asked if she should tell God that when she said wind she meant wind, not "WIND." I told her to leave God alone for he knew what he was doing. We were off north Sydney Head Light the following morning at 8:00 AM. Thank you God. (In all humility and thankfulness).

Again Janet used the handheld radio and called Sydney Radio. The operator shouted back, "Where are you?" Then a welcome voice came on frequency saying, "This is the New Zealand Naval vessel *Canterbury*. We have the yacht *Isle of Barra* in sight within 1/2 mile and are going to her assistance." We looked around and saw a gray boat streaking towards us. Quickly we lowered our sails and watched the *Canterbury* circling us with the sailors aboard cheering, waving, and taking pictures. We couldn't believe they were cheering us and we looked over out shoulder to see if they were waving at another vessel. They had been looking for us for five weeks.

The radio operator said that they were sending over a crew member to look at our steering. Then the captain came on the line and asked about our stores. Janet replied that we had enough to get us into Sydney but if they had an apple and a glass of cold milk it would sure taste good. We watched as they put an inflatable boat over the side, then two men went into the boat and were handed several boxes. They came to us over rough seas. The youthful engineer determined that our steering couldn't be fixed until we hauled out the boat. Then we opened the boxes. They had sent to us a case of apples, two gallons of fresh milk, two loaves of bread still warm from the oven, and two pounds of sweet butter. We scarfed it down. Then we called the *Canterbury* and said that no food had ever tasted so delicious. The captain replied, "It's only New Zealand's finest. Enjoy." That we did.

Sydney Radio called again and said that the Water Police boat *Nemesis* would come out the eight miles to tow us in and they would be accompanied by all the official boats. The *Canterbury* informed us that they had to leave for gunnery practice up north and another New Zealand naval vessel came into view. They stayed with us until an Australian naval vessel came to keep us company until the Water Police boat arrived. Upon arriving, the police boat threw us a line and began the tow into Sydney Harbor. We were followed by a veritable parade of boats: Immigration, Customs, and Medical personnel and many spectator boats, waving, blowing horns, and welcoming us to Sydney. We were towed in to the Cruising Yacht Club at Rushcutters Bay. The police tied us to a dock underneath a sign that said "Absolutely No Tying To This Dock". We were in Sydney Harbor after being adrift for 44 days and it felt very good. A total passage of 49 days from Fiji.

When the officials left all the media representatives came aboard. One TV reporter kept saying "1000 miles with no steering and you made it within 8 miles of Sydney! An incredible feat of seamanship. Incredible." Janet told him that the incredible thing was that after 49 days at sea, under rather trying conditions, she and her husband were still speaking to each other. That comment made TV that night.

During that conversation a very young newspaper reporter was visibly squirming. Finally he burst out,"Okay, I'm going to ask it. How old are you people?" Janet told him that to begin with she had shoes older than he was. Then she told him our ages. The next day in the paper we were referred to as elderly and older. Oh, well.

Because of the buildup of another storm (they call them Southerly Busters down there) the police couldn't tow us over to the marina where we had our reservations until the front had passed through. So we settled in to wait.

The Search and Rescue team out of Canberra, Australia wanted to interview us, to find out our condition, health etc., and if there was any information we might furnish that may be helpful in the future for their rescue operations. There were four men we invited aboard. The captain of the team asked most of the questions and another with pad and pencil took down all the information we furnished.

The first question by the Captain was, "Did you have an EPIRB aboard." EPIRB (Emergency Position Indicating Radio Beacon) This electronic devise when turned on is a line of sight radio, emitting an emergency signal, an SOS, Mayday, or distress signal that the Coast Guard can pinpoint the position and come to the rescue.

I said, "Yes, we had two on board. Right there, (pointing to the one in the cockpit) and we have another in our life raft."

The Captain then asked if we had turned either of them on.

"No." I said. "Neither of them were turned on."

"Why not?"

"Well, we had a dry boat (inside) and relatively, a healthy crew most of the time. During the worst of the storm Janet had fallen against the chart table and bruised or badly bent a couple of ribs and had to be immobilized for a couple of weeks. But other than that I saw no reason for turning on either of the EPIRBs." By turning on the EPIRB if a rescue was in the offing we would have had to abandon our boat. I asked the Captain, "Why should I have turned on the EPIRB under the conditions as noted?" He didn't give me an answer.

The Captain then asked about radio's, flares, and other signals.

My response was that we had given the "Pan, Pan, Pan" signal many times on the VHF radio. (A "Pan" signal is an emergency signal but not one of distress)

The Captain interrupted me and said, "We don't have VHF radio's on our search aircraft."

"Captain," I said, "Almost every boat in the Pacific and probably all the other oceans of the world have a VHF radio aboard. It would be reassuring to know your aircraft were equipped with VHF radio's for any future operation." A year later going up through the Great Barrier Reef, the little planes sent out by the government of Australia for Coastal Watch and

Rescues, were equipped with VHF radios, and we communicated daily with them.

I told the Search and Rescue team almost every important bit of information I could think of that happened during this trip, including the point that we were in touch with the Ham Radio Control Tony's Net, and that the day after the worst part of the storm, we had given our position and other data to them. I asked if this information had been passed on to them. The answer was in the affirmative.

"Then Captain," I asked, "You say you had this information, just where were you searching?"

"We were searching on the shores, rocks, and reefs of Lord Howe Island and Elizabeth Reef." the captain replied.

I almost lost my cool and said, "Good Lord what for?"

"Well we were looking for flotsam, debris and bodies," he replied a little harried.

"Captain," I said, "If your Search and Rescue team had taken our position given to you by Tony's Net, and drawn a straight line on your chart direct to Sydney and then made a search within five miles either side of that line you would have found us, or at least found the empty beer and wine bottles that we threw away."

I told the Search and Rescue team that when we had left Suva, Fiji, that eleven boats had left on the same day we did. We had heard on Tony's Net of one boat returning to Fiji after he had lost his mast. Two other cruising boats our size had gone to New Zealand and landed safely. Seven other racing boats from New Zealand had not showed up in port as of this time. Were they aware of those boats and did they know anything about them?

The captain said that the racing boats were very light displacement boats. Yes, they knew about them, had searched for them, but were afraid they were lost with their crews. (At the date of this writing I have never heard if any of the boats had shown in port or had ever been found.)

I firmly believe that a lot of good came of this interview.

Our stay at the Cruising Yacht Club was a delight. Very sociable and pleasant people. We used their telephones to call our son in Melbourne and took advantage of their hot showers. Then we went out to dinner. Janet found a large tree and gave it a very hearty hug. She said it felt good to be back on solid ground.

Three days later the Water Police towed us to Rabbit's Marina in Cammeray Bay. We went into our slip and made plans and reservations to fly to Melbourne to see our son and his family. Two days later we did just that.

After a week we returned to Sydney and prepared to fly back to the States. Our 3 1/2 month stay back in San Diego was great and we made one trip east to Colorado to visit my family. All in all it was good to be home. But we had to get back to Sydney to make boat repairs, and to continue on our trip.

Upon arriving back in Cammeray Marina where our boat was now moored, we made arrangements to haul the boat out to repaint the bottom and repair the steering and a multitude of things that the storm had damaged. The biggest expense and most trouble was having our diesel engine checked and discovering it could not be repaired. We would have to buy and install a new engine. The trouble was to find a reliable mechanic. The Marina and the Distributors of Perkins Diesel mechanics were booked for at least three weeks and couldn't possibly install. I knew simple maintenance but nothing about installation. I was given a card by the Marina office with the name of John Spry with several diesel and mechanical degrees after his name. The cost of a regular mechanic was $45.00 per hour. I wondered what the man with all the credentials would cost. I had to find out so called him. He said that before he took on any job that he would like to see the site and also that I could interview him. Me interview him! What kind of deal is this I wondered. Anyway I told him that I would pick him up in my dinghy as we were on a mooring.

The next day I picked up a seventy-ish year old man with beautiful snow-white bushy hair. The dinghy ride was short and as soon as we arrived on board my boat he wanted to see the site. "A piece of cake", he said and told me that he had been the top diesel mechanic for the entire Australian Army boats for 35 years and had been retired for some time and was now running his own mechanical shop.

I said to him, "Mr. Spry, with all due respect for your time, as I know you must be a very busy man, I must ask you what you charge per hour, as I am on somewhat of a limited budget, because the storm we were in did about $25,000.00 damage, so before I hire you we must come to an understanding.

Mr. Spry sent a chill through me as he smiled. I just knew I couldn't afford his price of labor. He stated very benevolently, "You know something, I like Yanks. If it hadn't been for America fighting in the southeastern Pacific, we Australians would be speaking Japanese today. What would you say if I charged you $15.00 an hour?"

"Mr. Spry" I said, "How soon can you start?" We were very fortunate in finding this man, a superb diesel mechanic who "liked Yanks" and who did a superior job of installing our new engine and getting it running. We shall always be grateful to John Spry.

I learned a new curse word from John. John would not say the usual expletives like damn or hell. His strongest and most obscene word was "Splendid!" If he dropped a nut or bolt in the bilge you knew he was disgusted with himself when he would say, "Splendid."

While the engine was out it was a good time to replace the hot water heater, repair several pumps and do some electrical wiring. The boat was a mess, tools lay around for easy reach, grease marks and dust here and there, our morale was at a low point because of all the work, cost and the interruption of our normal lives. We had weathered the storm, but would we weather the port conditions. It was touch and go until one day we heard a voice say, "May we come aboard?"

I looked in the direction of the voice and there was a small sailboat about twenty-four feet long. Aboard were two very nicely dressed people. The boat had an unbelievable amount of bird shit all over their deck. I said later that without all that bird shit all over their deck, I would never have invited them aboard, but if they could stand their boat the way it was, they sure as hell should be able to tolerate our boat with all the scattered tools, greasy rags etc. I invited them aboard.

It was instant friendship, the beginning of a wonderful relationship that has prevailed over the years with intentions of visiting each other in the future. James (not Jim) is an Englishman who went to Australia several years ago, met and married Merle, a native, and made friends with her family, twin boys. James was a computer and television executive and Merle was a music teacher in the greater Sydney area. Every time we heard her sing we would get goose bumps as she has such a rich and beautiful singing voice.

From the time they came aboard it was a very friendly greeting. Before they left that day we had wined and dined them, after we got a few tools put of the way. They lived very close, so we were together almost every day until we left Sydney. We went to many meals, musicals, concerts, picnics, parties, and spent the weekend in the Blue Mountains in their cabin. They and their circle of family and friends were of great importance to us.

We thoroughly enjoyed our stay in Sydney. We're very fond of Australia (they have the best seafood in the world) and many Australians became good friends. We traveled extensively, sometimes alone and sometimes with friends. All such a pleasure. Four friends from our yacht club in San Diego and two from the University of California, San Diego, came down to see us and we spent a wonderful Christmas with two of them.

With the advent of spring it was time to begin our passage north on the inside of the Great Barrier Reef. We had all the charts necessary to get us into the Mediterranean and with our two good Australian friends on board we prepared our departure. Our good friends James and Merle had intentions of buying a boat and sailing around the world, so we had invited them aboard to go as far as Brisbane, Australia to get a little experience. Early on April 12th we sailed out through the Sydney Heads where we had entered eight months before.

CHAPTER FOUR

When we left Sydney our two Australian friends James and Merle were aboard. They had sailed their small sloop in Sydney Harbor, but they had never sailed on the open ocean before so the rather rough waters of the Pacific as we cleared the Heads was an unpleasant surprise.

Within a few minutes Merle became very seasick and nothing seemed to help. We tried every kind of pill, pressure wrist band and a scopolamine patch behind the ear, with no relief. She didn't dare go below but was able to sit in the cockpit and sleep a little, then would awaken and be ill again. She felt she would get over this soon so we kept on going north. The next day James became seasick and it was evident that they wouldn't be able to go as far as Brisbane with us. We checked the chart and decided to put in at Coff's Harbor where they could catch a train and return to Sydney.

We picked up an end tie in Coff's Harbor and secured the boat. Our dear friends recovered quickly once on dry land and we bade them a sad farewell. They had sustained us during our stay in Sydney and we had shared so many good times, so tears were shed. James thanked us for saving them a small fortune in buying a cruising boat. Discovering their weak stomachs he said that they'd buy a chicken farm instead.

We stayed in Coff's Harbor for five days and then started once more for Southport, at the south end of Brisbane Bay. The channel into Brisbane Bay silts up rapidly and badly so it's necessary to contact the Volunteer Coast Guard by radio for them to guide you in safely. That we did. The Coast Guard boat arrived within 15 minutes and began to lead us down the channel. One of the officers assured us that the channel was a minimum of eight feet deep so there would be no problem. Wrong! Halfway to the Southport Yacht Club we were stuck aground. The Coast Guard boat came back and tossed us a tow line. Very apologetically the officer said "Our depth gauge showed eight feet."

Janet replied, "Ours didn't."

They towed us off the sand bar, and we motored the rest of the way into our assigned slip. It was a quiet place to stay and the club had a great dining room so we were looking forward to several nice days. Something else that made it very nice was meeting again fellow cruisers that we had first met in San Diego and again in Sydney. It was a bit of old home week. So we stayed an extra week in Southport and enjoyed every minute.

In leaving Southport Harbor, following the Coast Guard boat again, we touched bottom three times, but made it safely through the entrance. Once outside we stayed off shore about 10 miles. We wanted to continue to sail at night and you can't do that once you're into the inland passage of the reef, or even close to it. The Great Barrier Reef is just what it is. It is dotted with thousands of small reefs or islets, some only visible at low tide. The Reef is very poorly marked or not at all. One must be on guard at all times, so travel at night is not prudent. Some one had nicknamed it "The Great Barrier Grief." In the cases where there were just hulks, I can see why.

Once again a gale blew up and was right on our nose. So we had to motor or lose ground. This meant many hours for both of us at the wheel as the gale lasted for three days. We decided to go into Gladstone for a much needed rest.

We arrived off Gladstone and eyed the entry channel. It must be one of the longest entry channels in the world, but it's well marked with buoys and lights so you can't go astray. After that long trip it was with relief that we finally entered the river, but there were no moorings or dock space available. The harbormaster directed us to tie up on the outside of a line of three fishing boats. They didn't know what to do with a sailboat. Soon another trawler pulled in behind us. It was the *Hustler* out of Tweed Heads, about 300 miles south. The captain called over and asked if we would like some prawns. When we said "yes" he passed over about five kilos of king prawns. But that wasn't all, there were two dozen Moreton Bay bugs (shovel nosed lobster) and two large mud crabs. We invited the captain and his one man crew to dinner. After being at sea for five days they asked for time to clean up first.

Promptly on time they arrived polished, combed, and bearing a bottle of wine. It was one of the most memorable evenings we have ever spent in our cockpit. Janet had made a big salad, cocktail sauce for the prawns, and melted some butter for the lobster and crabs. "Speaking of dining in Lordly Splendor Wow!" When they left the captain kissed Janet on the cheek and said "God bless you." And we didn't even know their last names.

The harbor authorities moved us around many times, shuffling us between moorings and the dock. They really weren't prepared for cruising boats as the fishing trawlers came first.

We had problems with our depth finder and by inquiring around found an electronic shop doing this type of business. He diagnosed the transducer of our depth finder as the problem. Normally you would haul out to do the replacement. Not so here. At high tide (3:00 A.M.) we pulled the boat at the end of the dock with the bow as close to shore as possible and tied up. The Australians call this going on the grid. At low tide with our keel on hard sand and wading in about a foot of water the transducer was easily replaced.

When tying up to the end of the dock, I had tied the stern and headed to the bow to tie it, when I spotted the dirtiest, emaciated hungry looking Dalmatian dog I have ever seen. You could see every rib of the dog. I said, "Boy you are a mangy looking critter." With that he growled and came for my throat. I was kicking at him and yelled to Janet, "For God's sake, hand me the boat hook or something to fend him off." I reached back and Janet handed me the flare pistol–loaded. The dog was about three feet away and getting ready to lunge at me when I fired the pistol at point blank range. There was a loud bang, a brilliant flash of light and the missile sped directly between the dog's two front feet, glancing off the pavement, bouncing between the dogs hind legs, and on across a fence into a dry pasture setting it afire.

Needless to say the whole episode scared us both half to death.

"What happened to the dog?" Well the critter turned in mid-air and last we saw of him was running like a greyhound with his tail between his legs. At 3:00 A.M. I had to beat out the grass fire which only took a few minutes. I said, "Well so much for being an expert rifle and pistol shot, while in the Marine Corps."

When we left Gladstone we took the shorter northern channel out. Janet was at the wheel while I was on the bow sighting the buoys and the poles. You must follow the chart exactly and don't sneeze or you'll hit the reef. And don't try a shortcut. At last we were in the open ocean again...the western edge of the Tasman. After a few days of very light winds we pulled into Pine Island in the Middle Percy Isle Group and anchored. That night gale force winds came up and the anchorage got rough. They call it "The Percy Island Rock And Roll". Our anchor dragged, as did those of other boats, and we had to motor back to the anchorage against fierce winds.

From Pine Island we left with another boat and headed for Scawfell Island, sixty miles away. The winds were favorable and we made a very fast trip. In fact we got in so early and the anchorage was so relaxing that we invited our yachtie friends for dinner.

After 1 1/2 days we went north again heading through the Whitsunday Passage. We had to make a major course change and at midnight we were both in the cockpit discussing whether to make a sail change also. Suddenly there was a loud thud and the boat almost stopped and half twisted our boat around. There was a lot of water being splashed and loud thumping sounds against the boat. This was accompanied by loud moans and snorts like a whale blowing. The wind came up again and we began to move away. We looked back and could see water splashing and churning. Because of the darkness we couldn't see what we had hit, but assumed it was a sleeping whale. As our sails filled more we got out of there before the whale could figure out what it was that gave him a headache. It was no time for an apology.

We didn't stop at every harbor or island along the Australian east coast but we did stop at Magnetic Island and the East Bay of Great Palm Island on our way to Dunk Island. In East Bay a very near disastrous thing happened. According to the chart there was just one coral bommy (coral head) in the whole bay and we managed to hit it. To begin with we'd done what we said we'd never do, that is to go into an unknown harbor after dark. It wasn't night, but the sun was setting and the shadows of the mountains completely covered the bay. We couldn't see as we normally would an hour earlier.

We motored slowly in, watching the depth gauge carefully. It read 80 feet, then 75 feet, and then instantly, about five feet. We were on top of the bommy. The water was so clear that we could see it with our spreader lights, below our keel and there we sat. Janet put the engine in reverse and revved up the diesel. We didn't move an inch. I told Janet to quickly get the outboard cover off and loosen it while I was getting the dinghy over the side. My old adrenalin was flowing madly. I lifted the dinghy as if it were a feather, tossed it in the water, jumped in and tied the painter to the stern of our boat. I lifted the eighty five pound outboard as easily as a pillow, affixed it to the dinghy and gave the signal to Janet. With both motors going full blast in reverse, we revved the two motors and, in one concerted effort, pulled off the bommy without damage. Our new outboard motor and diesel engine had just paid for themselves. We went out and anchored in 72 feet of water and slept soundly.

Dunk Island was a very unstable anchorage and uncomfortable so we didn't stay long, but headed for the city of Cairns, just 20 miles away. By the way, Cairns is pronounced "Cannes," just like the city in France.

The river anchorage at Cairns was very pleasant. In town we were able to do major provisioning, take on fuel and water and have our 4000 watt generator rewound..to the tune of $600 Aus. I had only paid $300.00 U.S., for it when it was new. But, it was good to have refrigeration again.

While in Cairns I was exploring the river in our dinghy and was invited aboard a fishing vessel for a cup of coffee. I had only been aboard a few minutes when the fellow found that I was to be in Cairns for about a week. He pulled his car keys from his pocket and said, "Here are the keys to my car, take it and drive it while I'm gone. I'll be gone about ten days to two weeks so you may as well use it." You find greed, curiosity and generosity all around the world.

After leaving Cairns we were in the heart of the Great Barrier Reef. We had been skirting the Reef for over three hundred miles. There would be countless islands and reefs, but little else. If you run out of eggs up there, forget it. Now we would only be traveling during clear daylight hours.

Sometimes the passages through the reefs would be less than 100 yards wide, with the charts showing numerous wrecks along the way. Hardly encouraging. And some of the islands and reefs were poorly marked, if marked at all. So you have to be able to see where you were going. The cruising guides tell you to be anchored before 3:00 PM so you can see the reefs underwater. It really isn't difficult, but you must be cautious. And the scenery is worth it.

The last 300 miles, the York Peninsula, is aboriginal country and a forgotten world. No landing is permitted and you wouldn't want to anyway, because of the crocodiles. Occasionally we would see smoke from cooking fires and once saw a huge pillar of smoke coming from a runaway bush fire.

We were in the area of the large salt-water crocodiles. They are as much at home in the sea as on dry land. We saw a few and they give you the shivers. What you think is a log floating out there probably isn't. About a month before we arrived in crocodile country a young woman was killed and eaten by a crocodile. She had lived in that area for years and no one could figure out why she was swimming where she was. Her last swim was a big mistake.

Also we saw hundreds of poisonous snakes that were supposed to be very toxic. However, as they had such small mouths they weren't much of a threat to humans. I just didn't want any climbing up my anchor chain, and none did.

At Howick Island we saw mammoth turtles. They were

about three feet across and four feet long. Their heads were as large as a human head. Skittish, they wouldn't come near the boat.

Off Wharton Reef I caught a twenty pound Spanish Mackerel. My, they are good eating, as are the Coral Trout caught inside the reef. Once again we must say that the seafood in Australia is second to none. And that was about to be proved to us one more time.

Up to this time the weather along the coast had been mostly pleasant. Sure, there were a couple of bad spots but we overcame those and were able to sail every day. But now the weather really socked in. We ducked behind Night Island to get out of the Force 8 or 9 gale winds and anchored amidst several other cruisers and fishing boats who wanted cover. There was a large catamaran there named *Island Explorer* that was heading for Darwin to begin passenger service along the north coast of Australia. The captain called us on the VHF radio and invited us aboard for dinner. He even sent a dinghy to pick us up. That night we dined sumptuously on over one gross of raw oysters that they had just picked off the banyan tree roots. Then there was a small shark that was caught. Nothing much is wasted and in Australia shark when fried is called flake. There are no bones in shark and it is delicious eating. Janet had made a salad and bread pudding for dessert and that, combined with excellent company of the group, made for a great evening.

It was here that the little planes the Australian government used for "Coastal Watch" began to talk with us on the VHF radio. At first they wanted to know a few details of our boat, destination, etc. After that for the next three hundred miles we always got a pleasant, "Gd-day *Isle of Barra,* how's things going, etc." It was good to know in this God-forsaken area that there was some company around.

At Cape Grenville we were passed by an American destroyer on a goodwill tour of Australia. We talked briefly with them on the radio and learned that San Diego was still there despite an earthquake. Also heard that Baskin-Robbins still had thirty-one delicious flavors of ice cream. It was nice to hear an

American voice again.

We anchored at Margaret Bay near Hannibal Island on August 2, 1986. There were three other boats there, a sloop, a power boat and a small catamaran. The first two were Australian and the latter from New Zealand. They were long time friends and cruised together each year. They invited us to cruise with them to Thursday Island. This was an unexpected pleasure and we welcomed company. Much of this coast is very lonely and at one barren stretch we felt we were the only people left alive in the whole world. So we were looking forward to be traveling with this group. Besides being company, these boats had another advantage. The power boat and the catamaran were shallow drafted and could scout out harbors that were deep enough for the sailboats. We kept in touch via VHF radio.

On our way north we stopped at many small islands for a night's stay. The crews went ashore and beach-walked. The captains all carried powerful rifles, for crocodiles go beach-walking too. With the expertise in weaponry that I had shown in Gladstone with the Dalmatian dog, I may not have been as lucky facing a 20 or 30 foot crocodile. Fortunately we captains and the crocodiles did not meet.

All of us entered the Escape River behind Lizard Island after dodging all the sand bars. We anchored off a pearl farm where they cultivated cultured pearls. The firm was Japanese owned and had all Japanese workers. We invited them aboard for an evening of visiting and it was most interesting. Some of them had been there for six years earning money to get married and buy a home when they returned to Japan. One man was going to stay another four years and hoped his bride-to-be would still be waiting.

We had to stay in the Escape River for at least a week to wait for the proper tides to go through the channels to Thursday Island. The moon had to be just right. Otherwise the tides through the channels is sometimes better than 11 knots. So we settled in.

The crews of the boats got together every night for a pot luck supper and we enjoyed each other's company. During the day we read and fished. The elusive Burumundi were running, but I couldn't catch one. Not often do I get skunked. One Burumundi took my line, but he was like greased lightning. He ran my line out about fifty yards and snapped the line before I had a chance to snag him. That was the only bite I had.

These are the tasty fish that lure the crocodiles into the rivers and there were some small crocodiles around us. The Japanese workmen had to be in the water with them and they said they weren't very big, only about nine feet. That's big enough for us.

What did frighten the workmen were the sharks that came in. One afternoon a Japanese was fishing off the dock and he caught a fifteen foot long hammerhead shark. It was twisting around and about to tear out the dock so they shot it several times with a rifle. That didn't even seem to faze it. It finally bit through the chain holding it and got away.

Finally, according to the tidal charts, your bible while on the Great Barrier Reef, the moon and tides were in our favor so we and our good friends left our anchorage and headed north. We had planned on anchoring at Mt. Adolphus Island, but the catamaran radioed back a warning to us. They had 65 knot winds off the anchorage and all the boats in there were on the beach. So the rest of us did a sharp turn to port and entered the small cove at the nearest island. It was sheltered and calm and we stayed 1 1/2 days before heading out.

We dropped anchor at Horn Island and looked across the reef at the small settlement of this northernmost community of Australia–Thursday Island. We had stopped at many anchorages and seen some beautiful country, but now it was good to be back in civilization, small though it was. It was a long way from Sydney and we really felt that we had accomplished something.

CHAPTER FIVE

The small village on Thursday Island doesn't have too much to offer. But we were able to do some shopping for stores, have dinner out and sample some delicious ice cream. It was on that island that we had to say goodbye to our friends with whom we had shared the cruising of the York Peninsula. They were all going northeast to New Guinea and we were heading west for Bali. We had enjoyed their company so much and are grateful they invited us to join them.

Originally we had wanted to go up to the Solomon Islands. During World War II, the U. S. Marine Unit I was with had first landed on Guadalcanal (already taken over previously by another unit). Guadalcanal was only a training and reprovisioning area before my unit went into Bouganville, (my first taste of actual combat). However, while we were in Pago Pago, American Samoa, we had heard that there had been an outbreak of malaria that was so insidious that people that had health problems, such as respiratory, diabetes, heart problems etc., should give the islands a wide berth. I guess that the disease given by the anopheles mosquitoes to humans had built up such an immunity that short of a miracle, people died very quickly. So this bypass was a must.

Once more we had to intently study the tidal charts, for leaving Thursday Island is almost as bad as getting there. The tidal currents flow very swiftly through the western channels and you have to hit them at just the right time. We got fuel and water and, in the company of a 65 foot long German ketch and a 36 foot Swiss sloop, we prepared to leave the Torres Straits.

In that section of the world the tides are very strange. You are between the Arafura Sea and the Pacific Ocean and their tides conflict. It may be high tide in one spot and 30 miles away it will be low tide. So you have just a few short hours to get through the channels and into the Straits before the tides change again. Otherwise you are swept backwards. The tides were several feet and caused very swift currents, sometimes as much as seven knots.

The German boat had big, powerful engines and he said he'd go through the channels first and would radio back to us. If we needed help he would come and get us. We made it through okay, passing the rusting hulks of those boats who didn't. You must motor out at least 50 miles from Thursday Island to get out of the tides and currents. So motor we did; the wind was very light but with our big sails up it helped a little.

After we had motored the prescribed distance, the wind died completely. All of the crews were tired of motoring so we decided to drop anchor and get some sleep until the wind came up. Don't forget, we were in the middle of the Arafura Sea, but it was only 30 feet deep. We turned on anchor lights and went to bed. About four hours later the wind came up and we all raised sails again.

Once more we said goodbyes as the other two boats were going to Darwin, Australia, and we were about to turn north to Indonesia.

Our sail along the islands of Indonesia was charming. It wasn't very fast, about 5 knots, but it was gale-free and the islands were beautiful. We stayed about 40 miles off the island of Timor for they are having a civil war there. The Seven Seas Cruising Association's Commodore's Bulletins said to give it a wide berth. It seems they tend to shoot at you and ask questions later if you get too close.

Once we rounded Sumba Island and turned more northwesterly, we were caught up in a current that swept us west past the channel leading to Benoa, Bali. We had to turn on the diesel and motor east. A scary thing then happened. About 1/2 mile off our starboard beam, the lights of a large freighter suddenly appeared. He was going parallel to us, but we hadn't seen him at all. He went on about another 1/2 mile then turned out his lights again. That's a very dangerous practice.

At dawn the next morning we were entering the channel between Bali and Lombok islands. The swells were very high and we were literally surfing in. Alongside the boat were dozens of dolphins enjoying the ride also. Leaving the main channel and entering the Benoa, Channel is very tricky. Yes, it's well marked, but once again you don't dare sneeze. The harbor was small and crowded, but we found a spot and anchored. Then, with the ships papers, I went to clear us in.

At that time getting a cruising permit for Indonesia was difficult. You could apply, send your money, and then might never hear from them. They also kept your money. So we did what so many cruisers did, we went in without a permit and paid for a three day stay. And that was our first experience with *baksheesh*, or officials with their hands out. Because we were Americans and all Americans are millionaires, you know, we had to have $100 tucked into each passport. The British got by with $20 and the Aussies just $5.

While there we did take several tours–going to see the temple dancers, which were marvelous, and then further out on the island to all the shops and the monkey park. While on these tours our agent was refueling our boat or having someone do it. A big, big mistake on my part for not being there and overseeing as they refueled. Live and learn, and to our regret we learned much later.

The open market had wonderful produce and we really stocked up. For about $40.00 U.S. I purchased enough provisions to last for several days. The only real problem was with the bank and my master card. They would only give me a cash advance of $200.00 per week. That really put a crimp in our usual tourist spending spree. However, with the provisions we didn't need anything else.

We could have got an extension to our three day stay if we had given the young naval officer in charge of extensions more money or some cigarettes or Playboy magazines. After paying for fuel we were short of cash and had none of the other two items, so we left.

Once outside the main channel and into the Timor Sea

there was another strange happening. We could hear the sound of surf although there were no islands in sight. Then looking to our stern we could see surf coming towards us. It was about 18 inches high and stretched for miles. It would sweep on past and all was calm, and then, in about 20 minutes, we would hear it again and along would come another line of surf. When this surf swept by us you would think you were in a raging river current. This continued for two days and then stopped. When we got into Flying Fish Cove on Christmas Island, the boat that left Benoa, the day after we did had the same experience. The boat that left two days later didn't know what we were talking about.

Making a landfall is always a thrill, and Christmas Island was no exception. It loomed up all by itself and we were at last in the Indian Ocean. It was night when we got there, and we couldn't find the entrance to the cove; however we had no intentions of going into port at night. We were blinded by the lights of the big boats at the docks that were taking on phosphate. So we kept cruising back and forth about two miles off. Suddenly a voice came over the VHF Channel 16 (we always turn it on when we sight another boat or are near the entrance of a harbor). The voice said it was calling the sailboat cruising back and forth off shore. We answered and he said he was the captain of the sailing yacht *Sagan* and he would talk us into the cove. He turned on his masthead strobe light, warned us about the huge mooring buoys for commercial vessels, and talked us straight into the anchorage. He had arrived the night before, having been talked in himself and was returning the favor. What a nice thing to do. And it was quite a job for him as he had been eating dinner in a restaurant way up the hill when he saw our running lights. So he ran down the hill to the anchorages, leaped into his dinghy, rowed out to his boat and called us. We were most grateful.

Little Christmas Island is pretty much closed down now. We understand that the phosphate has given out and most of the workers are gone. They were in the early stages of closing when we were there in 1986. There was still good shopping at the supermarket and several good restaurants. Also the small yacht club was most hospitable. Unfortunately there was a strike on when we were ready to leave and we couldn't buy more than 25 gallons of fuel. We had to buy the diesel fuel from the supervisors, which I think was beneath their dignity. Also the water was contaminated and had to be either boiled or treated before drinking it.

Using Ocean Passages Of The World as our guide, we plotted our course to Galle, Sri Lanka. Those in the know say the Indian Ocean is the most uncomfortable ocean in the world and we must rank it up there pretty high. There wasn't much wind, but the seas were very active. It was a bumpy ride. Then the winds died completely, and we went into a flat calm.

The fuel we had taken on in Bali was filthy and by the time I strained it we had just 27 gallons left. That included the 25 gallons from Christmas Island. So we just sat in one spot and bobbed around except for that hour when we ran the engine to charge the batteries and then we went about six miles. After 10 days of this we really wanted to get going. So Janet put out a CQ call on the HAM radio. She said, "CQ, CQ, CQ to any sailing vessel in the Indian Ocean." A CQ call means for anyone to come in.

Finally a rather bored voice said, "To the vessel calling CQ, this is the schooner *Saudade*, may I help you?" Janet asked if he had a weather fax aboard and told him we had been sitting in one spot for nine days, gave him our position, and said that we needed some wind. He did have a weather fax and said that we should get some wind the following day as there was a low approaching. Then he asked if we had any more problems. Janet told him that we were low on fuel, but we would make it okay. She thanked him for his help and they both signed off. Suddenly HAM radio stations from all over Asia were coming on frequency saying that they were standing by if we needed any help. Janet commented on how nice people were.

The next morning she tuned up to call Rowdy's Net out of Hong Kong to give them our report for health, wind, position etc., as we normally did, when she heard a voice say "Has anyone heard from N6EZI?" As that's the call sign we use she jumped in and said "This is N6EZI." The voice said "Janet, this is Don Hopper from Tony's Net (the one in the southwest Pacific). Where are you so we can come rescue you?" Startled Janet said, "We don't need rescuing. What's this about?"

Don Hopper answered, "They interrupted the southeast Asia Net last night and said that the yacht *Isle of Barra* was out of food and water. Then someone came in and said "she's diabetic and is probably out of insulin too." Janet assured Don that we had enough food for six months, had caught 80 gallons of water in a rainstorm a few days before, and she had a two year supply of insulin.

Don asked her to stay on frequency and please tell that to the man in charge of rescues for the Indian Ocean. He came on from Perth, Australia, and Janet repeated her story. Then he laughed heartily. He told her to brace herself, for 23 oil tankers had been diverted from their courses and were on their way to our last known position to bring supplies, the P and O liner *Canberra* was steaming to our assistance and they were flying a plane out of Diego Garcia to drop us supplies.

Janet yelled, "Call 'em off, call 'em off! We don't need anything!" We'll never know if they were kidding or not, but fortunately the wind came up and we moved north. Our best guess is that when Janet said we were low on fuel, the other HAM operators thought she said food. And if out of food, then they also assumed short on water. And they just threw in the insulin bit to be helpful. So enunciate clearly when you talk on the HAM radio. What a wonderful instrument the HAM radio and the system of people that participate in all the activities.

We went north rather slowly and crossed the equator again. We were anxious to reach Galle, Sri Lanka, but our timing was bad. It was night when we neared the island. Having been warned that many of the lights marking the channel into the harbor were out, we didn't dare try to enter. Instead we circled until daylight, dodging huge freighters the entire time, and then entered. Some of those large freighters apparently didn't like the idea of entering the harbor at night and now were entering either just ahead or behind us. We picked up a mooring buoy on a stern line and dropped a bow anchor. Then I went in to clear with the authorities.

Now was our introduction to Don Windsor, the yacht agent at Galle. For a modest fee he does all your paper work for you and arranges for any work you might need done. Also available are trips and tours all over the southern half of the island. We were there at the peak of the Tamil Tiger rebellion, but we never once felt threatened. The harbor was quite secure with armed guards all around keeping an eye on everything.

Each night Don Windsor and his wife turned their home over to all the cruisers and a served a delicious curry dinner for a very low price. There were also hot showers to be had and Don would arrange for special purchases to be made. Since we were there in 1985 Don has died, but his daughter and one of his sons continues with the business of being agents. They are a lovely family.

We made several trips to the capital city of Colombo and each time stayed at the magnificent Galle Face Hotel. The oldest hotel in Sri Lanka, it is one of the last vestiges of the British Raj–old world service and comfort in an elegant setting. Celebrities from all over the world have stayed there: kings, queens, prime ministers, presidents, lords. dukes etc. We even had some royalty from the U.S.: Duke Ellington and Count Basie. Their names were engraved on a large polished brass plate hanging in the lobby. The dining room overlooked the Indian Ocean, and there was one waiter who could have passed for Gunga Din had Gunga Din really lived. We loved every moment we spent there and hope to go back some day.

We would go to our room and before I could find my key, a brown hand had unlocked the door to let us in. Always it seemed an unnoticeable but ubiquitous servant was there ahead of you, anticipating every need you had. We would go into our room, smell the fresh flowers in the vase, pour us some water with ice cubes, maybe help ourselves to a beer, coke or whiskey if we wanted. Take a bath in a tub big enough for both of us to swim together at the same time. Take an afternoon nap. About five P.M. we would get dressed go down to the bar and have a Singapore Sling and watch the sunset. Before too long, when our Matre'd saw that our drink was about gone, he came up quietly and said. "Sahib, your table is ready."

We would follow the barefooted Matre'd (Gunga Din) to our table. Janet would order the bouillabaisse and I a top sirloin steak and wine. The bouillabaisse comes in a bowl almost as big as a bushel basket. I could see crab hanging on the sides of the bowl with huge hunks of fish, clams and other sea foods in the soup. Janet's immediate reaction was, "My Gawd! I can't eat all that."

I said, "Gee that is too bad!" and helped her dispose of the huge chunks of seafood, along with my delicious steak. The cost was so modest that we could go there every day of the week.

We would go back to our room and find our room had been serviced with a new vase of flowers, all new linen–the bed re-made and clean towels, a fresh pitcher of water and more ice cubes, and any drinks in the refrigerator replaced.

No wonder royalty and celebrities loved the place. You sure as hell don't need a television in a place like that.

While provisioning and shopping, we hired one of the three wheel taxi cabs to take us to and from the agent's office and Galle which was about two miles. The first taxi drivers charged us 65 rupees and we didn't think any thing about the price. Cheap fare. Then one evening we caught a taxi showing "Sarath" as the owner and driver. On debarking I paid him the 65 rupees. Immediately Sarath handed back 50 rupees, with the remark that 15 rupees was the fare and he wouldn't take more, not even a tip.

We reported this to Don Windsor. He said, "I must interview him, sometimes you meet someone that is completely honest." Eventually Don made the interview and said that he was one of a kind and put him on his list as recommended cabbies.

Damn it! I would open my big mouth. Now it was rare when we could get him. But fortunately we had gotten some publicity in the Colombo News Paper with photographs. Sarath kept looking for us and gave us top priority in his cab for regular rides and day long tours, He had our pictures and newspaper clipping attached to the dashboard and proudly pointed out to all his clientele that we were his customers. We were celebrities.

One Sunday Sarath invited us to his village about five miles north of Galle. Bright and early he picked us up as we were to spend the whole day. First we stopped at the Buddhist temple at his village where his brother was a monk. I was going to take a picture of Sarath, Janet, and the monk, but the school at the temple had just let out. When the picture was finally snapped it also included 40 Sri Lankan children.

When we arrived at Sarath's home, all the little wide eyed children followed. Sarath was proud as a peacock. He said, "You two are the first Europeans to ever visit my village." No wonder the little kids were wide eyed. They had never seen a European. All foreigners were Europeans to those humble people.

Sarath took us into his home and introduced us to his wife Chandrika, a beautiful shy woman, and then to her mother, various uncles, cousins etc. There must have been two dozen or more in the house. But his proudest moment was introducing his 39-day old son to us. For some reason it seemed very appropriate and I was encouraged to hold Dilan on my lap, with his little head by my knees. Dilan's itty bitty little hands barely circling my little fingers. Dilan was lying there, cooing and laughing at me, and was peeing all over my lap. His parent were so embarrassed.

I tried to ease the situation by ignoring my wet pants and by saying to his father, "Sarath your son was born to be a politician. Who else do you know that can laugh at you and piss on you at the same time without making you mad at him."

We had some wonderful times with Sarath and his family and even had to pose at the photographer for a family portrait as they had adopted us as Dilan's godparents. It was difficult leaving this wonderful family. Sarath said that when Dilan graduated from college that we would have to come see him graduate. We told Sarath that we would be very old and that we might be in a wheel chair. "Oh! Dilan will push you," he said.

It was now time to sweat out the monsoon season. We had to wait for the wet one to end and the dry one to begin. Unfortunately the dry one was late so it was just a few days before Christmas that we were able to leave. Bombay was to be our next stop. We were looking forward to that for we wanted to go to Agra and see the Taj Mahal and fly to Katmandu, Nepal. So up went the sails and we headed west around the southern tip of India.

Once again the winds were rather spotty so we didn't make much speed. And there were Indian fishing boats all over the place. With engines going at top speed they would head straight for us holding a fish in the air. We didn't know if they were just showing their catch or trying to sell it, but we'd have to turn on our engine to get out of their way. One dark night we were sailing along when suddenly all around us lights came on. There must have been 100 or more fishing boats who had seen our running lights and we had to zigzag between them.

Because most of the Indians cook their food on open fires the whole coast of India is covered with a smoky haze. Visibility was cut to just a few hundred yards off shore. And you can smell the wood burning from quite a way at sea. Not too unpleasant and it did tell us we were close to land.

It was almost dusk when we entered Bombay Harbor and we soon lost the channel lights in the glare of the lights on shore. Janet tried to contact the Bombay Pilots on the VHF radio, but there was no answer. So rather than do something stupid, like run into something, we pulled in between two of the huge freighters anchored in the harbor. We dropped anchor in 30 feet of water, ate dinner and went to bed.

The next morning we could see the archway marking The Gateway Of India about two miles away. In front of it was the only yacht harbor and that's where we were going. After breakfast we motored over and met another cruising friend that we had known in Sri Lanka. He told us where to anchor and we did. Then with our papers I went in to check in with the authorities. I told them that we had come in the night before and anchored, but nothing was said.

When I returned we went in to the Royal Bombay Yacht Club. It is a most impressive building with another touch of elegance. This is one of the most hospitable clubs we visited during our circumnavigation. The members welcomed us openly and warmly, issuing many invitations. Their hospitality made us feel like members. So many invitations were given, in fact, that we had to turn many down. We didn't feel we could eat three or four lunches and that many dinners in one day. But we did accept the offers of tours around the city and various parties.

The facilities of the club are exceptional and we took advantage of them. One day we were seated in the lovely lounge when a member came by and said, "Congratulations. America has just won the America's Cup back." That was good to hear.

Once we were talking to a member at the club about the difficulty we had with some people and the language barrier. He said, "If you can speak Hindi, you can go any place in India and get by fine. However, if you can speak English you can go anyplace in the world." We found that remarkably true. We had some difficulty in the past, but we had gotten this far and made lots of friends of many nationalities and languages.

Through our Sikh friends at the yacht club, we were invited to a Hindu wedding. From our anchorage in the bay we had seen the pre-wedding processions on shore and had wondered about them. Now we were to see one up close. The wedding was to be held in a large hotel in the center of Bombay and the groom was escorted to the location by a band wearing a tower of gas-fed lights on their heads. There were many dancers and we waited to catch sight of the groom. We were told that at Sikh weddings the groom rode to the proceedings on a white horse, but this groom arrived in a Volkswagen bug. Hardly as romantic, but the bug did take him to the hotel to meet his prospective male in-laws. After his acceptance by them, everyone adjourned to the wedding being held in an upstairs room.

It was February in Bombay, but the weather was very hot and the upstairs room was even hotter. The bride and groom were on a small stage under a canopy. In the middle of the stage was a fire continually being fueled by Hindu priests throwing in cups full of *ghee,* which is the clarified butter used in so many Indian recipes and it burns furiously. As the bride was dressed in a dark red sari made of heavy material and many, many pounds of gold ornaments, she must have been dying of the heat. The groom didn't look too comfortable either.

After all the invited guests had paraded past the bridal couple for introductions, the crowd adjourned downstairs for dinner while the wedding ceremony went on. In fact, it went on and on—for three more hours. We understand that it was one of the shorter ceremonies. But it was a great experience and we're so glad we had it. It was at this wedding that we met the consul-general of the American Legation. It was a most fortunate meeting as we would later have to call on him for help.

Our planned trip to Agra and Katmandu was not to be, for Indian officialdom interfered. The other American captain met us in the lounge one day and gave us a bit of news. He said he'd just heard something funny. He and his crew and the two of us were suspected of being spies for Pakistan. We laughed–and we shouldn't have.

Early the following Monday an Immigration boat came alongside. It was doing about 10 knots and really clipped us. The officer said we had to fill out more papers for they had lost the ones I had filled out before. That we did and he left. Then another boat banged into us. They were Customs and had also lost our papers, so we had to fill out more.

The other American captain on the yacht *Magic* and I left to go into town, and Janet went below to take a shower. Then Kaboom!, another boat rammed us. A male voice called, angrily, "Get out here!" Janet asked who he was and he just shouted louder, "Get out here!" She said that she would as soon as she put on some clothes. She went out into the cockpit to confront a very angry young naval officer standing on the deck of a small gun boat.

He waved his arm at all the freighters in the harbor and shouted, "Which of those boats are you with?" Janet said we were with none of them. Then he pointed at the other American boat and shouted, "You are with them!" Janet said we were alone. Then he shouted again, "You're both Americans so you are together!" Janet explained to him that the other boat was from Hawaii and we were from California. He didn't seem to understand.

Then, without asking permission, he waved two sailors aboard our boat and he followed them below. Janet watched and said later that they didn't open any thing and were out in a few minutes. Then they left aboard their own boat and went over to the other American yacht. but the first mate wouldn't allow them aboard.

There were five or six official boats every day. Each boat was generally 55 to 65 feet in length and very heavy. When they came at 5 knots and banged into you there was a resounding thud and you felt like you eye teeth would drop out. There were several dings and holes that had to be covered with fiberglass. Several stanchions were bent or broken and had to be replaced. All this at our own expense. There was other minor damages that made us furious but there was nothing much we could do.

The boats full of officials kept arriving every day until Friday. And we filled out more papers each day, duplicating what we had done the day before, and the day before that, etc. On Friday the Harbormaster came aboard when we were being visited by one of our unwelcomed official boats. He was a friend and we'd had dinner with him the night before. He pretended he didn't know us and asked Janet if she would show him below. Once there he thanked her for not losing her cool and added that he didn't know the reason for all this harassment for he could find out nothing. But he advised us not to go on any trips for the officials might tow the boat away. Or, if they wanted in and we weren't there, they might take an axe to the hatch.

We had accepted invitations through the next Thursday so canceled all of our travel plans and planned to stay through that day. Early Friday morning I went to all the necessary official offices to clear port. In the afternoon we went in to the open market and the grocery stores to stock up on food. When we returned to the Yacht Club, we found two uniformed men with sidearms waiting for us. They asked me to go with them right now. I refused, and said to them, "When I get my wife and all the groceries aboard then I'll go with you."

Then the men asked for our passports. I refused again. Determinedly the men then said I would have to come with them without further ado.

I stuck out my arms with wrists together and told them to put on handcuffs and take me and when he got to where they were going I planned on raising so much hell that they'd be sorry. The men backed down and said that I could get Janet and all the food on board and they would watch until I returned. Aboard the boat Janet kissed me goodbye and I told her I would see her later.

It was 4 1/2 hours before I returned to a very nervous Janet. I told her our passports had been impounded, our port clearance revoked, and that we were detained for interrogation on Monday. About fifty yards off, a small gun boat had anchored and was manned and armed with a machine gun pointing in our direction.

The following day all of our Indian friends at the Yacht Club told us to get to the American consul-general immediately.

That we did. We told the consul-general our story, and he got on the telephone and began dialing. It took him several hours before he was able to contact the police commissioner for all of India. He talked for several minutes and then said, "Spies! They're not spies! They're old!" Janet asked if he couldn't have phrased that more delicately. But he did get the interrogation moved up to that afternoon instead of on Monday, three days later.

We returned to the Royal Bombay Yacht Club where our Sikh friend introduced us to a nice Englishman that he said was going to our interrogation with us. We were not too impressed with him until he took us to the CID Office in a chauffeur-driven car. We still did not realize the importance of this British gentleman.

Our Sikh friend went with us to the interrogation, but would not go into the building. He said the Sikhs had been blamed for the assassination of a very high official, and now, although he himself was a high official, he did not want to jeopardize our chances with his presence. He would send his British friend in a few minutes, but for us to go on in the building.

When we walked into the office we faced about 20 men sitting behind a row of desks, who were glowering at us. There wasn't a smile anywhere. The apparent director of the interrogation pointed to two chairs in front of a table for us and told us to sit down. Shortly thereafter the Englishman walked into the room and all of the glowering men leaped to their feet. With smiles, they offered coffee, tea or cold drinks. The Englishman just chewed on his pipe and said, "I'm here as a friend of the McNeills." The McNeills found that incredible for they had just met him. But the whole atmosphere in the room had changed from malevolence to benevolence. Almost!

Then the interrogation began. For 2 1/2 hours they asked questions trying to pinpoint the time that we crossed the main channel after anchoring in the harbor for the night.

"After breakfast." was our answer.

"What time did you eat? How long did it take? What did you cook? How long did it take to fix it?" It was a futile questioning for neither of us had looked at a watch. But it seemed very important to the CID team to know the exact minute the channel had been crossed.

That line of questioning finally ended and the director pulled some papers from a drawer and read from them. "You've been accused of going to all the secret places in Bombay Harbor in your dinghy on February 2nd at 10:00 A.M."

Janet said "We have the only red rubber dinghy in all of Bombay. Don't you think we'd have flunked spying if we had gone all over the harbor especially to the secret places that you say on that day? There must have been at least 10,000,000 people on and around the shores and in boats on that sunny Sunday."

The director looked startled for a moment, then reached inside his desk and handed over our two passports and wrote out a new port clearance. He offered no apologies, but dismissed us. We fled back to the yacht club and said goodbye to all our Indian friends. Our Sikh friend tenderly took Janet's hand in his and said, "Janet, just think of this as part of your great adventure." Perils of Pauline? Ha! That's Janet's middle name. Then we topped off our fuel and water tanks and raised anchor quickly.

By the way, the British man that changed the whole attitude of the interrogation was not just the ordinary "Brit." His name was Mr. Grant. Mean anything to you? Well it didn't mean anything to me either until I read the card that he had given me. It said, "Manager of Gulf Oil of Indian Ocean, and the Red Sea". All I have to say is if you are going to hobnob with the great, you have to go to the top. I'm positive, even though he didn't say anything in our defense, his presence was very influential to our benefit. Thank you Mr. Grant.

While sailing out of the harbor, we were trying to think of some reason for it to be so important to know what time we crossed the main channel on the way to the yacht harbor. Then we remembered that we had seen a nuclear submarine on the surface heading out to sea. It had no flags or numbers, but we could see men on the vane. We asked an Indian naval officer at the yacht club about nuclear vessels. He said they had none. Then we said that they allowed their friends (namely Russia) to bring in their nuclear vessels. He vehemently denied this. If it was so secret, then why was one on the surface on a sunny day? Fortunately we had forgotten it and didn't mention it when being interrogated by the CID. They'd have hanged us by our thumbs. A year later we read in the newspaper that India admitted to having a Russian submarine on lease so they could train Indian sailors. So much for deception.

Those rotten officials had done us out of the Taj Mahal and Nepal, which were the only reasons we went to India to begin with. Well, you can't win them all.

CHAPTER SIX

The sail across the Arabian Sea was a pleasure and we needed that after Bombay. The seas were smooth and the winds constant although not heavy. We breezed along at about 5 knots as we relaxed completely.

While passing by the southern end of the Persian Gulf we saw our first super tankers. They are massive and look like a city afloat. We viewed them fearfully as they neared. Then gave a sigh of relief as we saw their bow angle change just enough to miss us. And that they did.

The Arabian Sea is full of animal life. Much of it was so strange that we thought they were from some horror movie or at least another planet. At one point the water around the boat was full of unknown creatures. Almost jellyfish-like in appearance they were various colors and shapes. Most were huge and elongated. We'd never seen anything like them before or since.

When we sighted the shores of the Sultanate of Oman we were startled to see how much it looked liked Arizona. There were high buttes and mesas in view with colors the same as Arizona. The only things that told you that you weren't anywhere near Yuma were the waves beating on the shore and the camels walking around. Definitely not southwestern USA.

According to the Sailing Directions we were to ask permission to enter the port of Mina Raysut on the southern coast of Oman and the port for the city of Salalah. So when about two miles away Janet called on the VHF and talked with the harbor master. He gave permission to enter and told us to anchor in the center of the harbor where two other sailboats were anchored.

Then he said, "Welcome to Oman." We'd never been welcomed anywhere before and it was nice to hear.

Shortly after we dropped anchor a police boat came alongside and two very polite policemen told us to stay aboard our boat and the officials would come out to us on the following morning. And they did, complete with turbans and long robes. With excellent manners and kindness, they filled out all of the required papers for us to enter Oman and then departed in their dinghy. Our passports went with them to be kept at the police station at the main entrance to the harbor.

Janet had an infection on her back and needed to see a doctor about it. I had refused to let her have it lanced in Bombay because of the filth everywhere there. I felt that even the air was full of germs. We had been told to go to Oman where all the doctors were Egyptians and were British trained.

About half way between Bombay and Oman, Janet asked me to lance the cyst, infection or what ever it was as it was about the size of a hens egg. Janet had a terrible time sleeping, was in constant pain, and was white as a sheet. I was reluctant to lance it in fear of doing muscle or nerve damage or spreading the infection further. I wasn't about to start any incision until I had read everything in the textbooks.

It was mid-afternoon when I did give Janet some local anesthesia around the infected area. Taking a sterile scalpel in hand, I started the procedure. By the time I had incised about one half inch, I was shaking like a leaf and sweat poured from my brow. I said, "I'm terribly sorry honey, but I just can't do any more. All that is coming out is a little blood, and I'm afraid to go any further. You will just have to bear the pain until we get to Oman."

I gave her some pain pills which didn't help much. She was in terrible agony–couldn't sleep, rest, or anything. I took over most of her duties.

So we picked up our passports and went in to the town of Salalah and the Qaboos Hospital–named for the Sultan. Janet went to the women's ward and saw the doctor. He was Egyptian and had trained in Britain. He examined the infected area and asked who had been fooling with it. The doctor told us that I had done everything right except that I didn't go deep enough. I told him, "Yeah! Well I did a good clean job–look at the messy job you are making."

The Middle Easterners do not have much of a sense of humor. He only smiled a little and told Janet to return in two days. When I went to the cashiers office to pay the bill, I told the clerk kiddingly that I might not have enough money to pay. The clerk said, "Your wife can't have the operation unless you pay first." I told him she'd already had the operation. He repeated that we had to pay. I then said that if we didn't have enough money, would he take Janet as a hostage? The poor clerk was twisting his hands and looked as if he would cry. Then I paid the bill in full. The entire cost of all this was about $7.00US.

Then I said to the clerk, "Now that I paid you, I do get to keep my wife, don't I?" Not one smile from the clerk as if to say. "You must pay before the operation."

In the hospital Janet saw a very tall man dressed all in white with boots, turban and bandoleers of shells crossing his chest. On his waist he wore a J-shaped knife in a sheath. Janet asked one of the nurses who he was. She replied that he was from one of the mountain tribes and no one fooled with them. That was understandable.

We were impressed with the town of Salalah. It was squeaky clean. The people were very friendly. As a country, Oman is a police state. It seems that the Saudis and Yemenis keep trying to invade the rich little sultanate, so they stay prepared. There are armed guards around the harbor, but we never felt intimidated. And the gate is guarded by the police. Each time we would pick up our passports to go in to town the policeman would hold up his hand and stop the next car going out the gate. He'd say "Take these people in to town!" Then the poor Arab driver would have to clean off his front and back seats and make room for us.

I don't think the young policemen knew how to read, or at least read English. There were only a couple of boats in the harbor and they only had about six or at the most eight passports in the office. It would take about half an hour for them to find our passports. I caught them a couple of times peeking around the corner trying to match our faces to the faces on the passports.

I had been seeing some big fish around the boat that should be good eating, but couldn't catch them for lack of the right kind of bait. I decided that if I had a few small fish I could use them, resulting in pan size fish. I took my small fishing gear and went over to the dock to catch the small fish. After a few moments a hand was placed on my shoulder and I heard the words, "No fish. No fish."

A soldier with a rifle was pointing to the Police Headquarters, I told him in gestures it didn't matter, then took my fishing gear and went back to our boat. The next day I took my fishing gear back to the dock and walked up to a different sentry, and tapped him on the shoulder. The sentry turned around to see an outstretched arm ready for a very friendly handshake. The sentry smiled and took my hand. He spoke a little English. I asked him if it would be all right to catch a few small fish from the dock and the reason why.

To my surprise the sentry was most congenial. The sentry said, "Sure, O.K. to fish, bring your scuba gear. Bring spear gun. Take all want." It goes to prove a handshake goes a long way. I then caught a couple small fish, took them back to the boat, but try as I might, the big fish wouldn't bite.

Here in Oman, ten thousand miles from home, I desperately needed money to buy supplies and fuel. Although the clerks at the bank were very friendly, my Master Card was not made on the Bank of Hong Kong. I made a very expensive telephone call to my trust officer in San Diego for money with instructions on how the money was to be sent. The only way was to get a certified check sent from San Diego through a bank in New York. We waited for several days and then called home to find out if my trust officer had sent the money and how. My trust officer said that the check should have been there as it was an electronic transmission. I had to go back to San Diego about six months later and found that the check had just returned to my trust officer. Some bank officials somewhere made a few bucks of interest on my long lost check, I bet.

In desperation, I described our plight to an Englishman who had arrived from Bahrain. He cashed a personal check for a few hundred just so we could get by. Believe me that gesture was very much appreciated.

There were many camels in Oman; some were fenced in, tied, or hobbled, but most were roaming around freely including the highways. Woe be it unto you if your car hit one and maimed or killed it. Even though you were a passenger, you may be held responsible because of the driver's speed. The driver or you could be held responsible to pay the equivalent of $25,000.00US or more for a camel's death. The camel was worth more than a human. If you caused a human death, you might be fined only $10,000.00US.

The town of Salalah (seven miles from the harbor) doesn't have much to offer but there was an open market for fruits and vegetables and one small grocery store for canned products. We bought what we needed and enjoyed our short stay there. Then it was time to go west again this time to the port of Aden in what was then The People's Democratic Republic of Yemen. In other words a communist state.

The Seven Seas Cruising Association Commodore's Bulletins had said that for about 30 miles out of Oman the SATNAV (Satellite Navigation Systems) does not work. No one knows why, a phenomenon of nature, but they just won't work. The Bulletin was right. For many westward miles the SATNAV was dark. Then suddenly the lights came on and we got a position.

The weather south of the Arabian peninsula could have been improved upon. There were many squalls, and one night a squall of about 70 knots plowed into us. We heeled over so hard that sea water poured into two open ports on the port side and the cockpit. I was on watch and I yelled at Janet (who was asleep) to close the ports. She did and took the wheel as I lowered the sails. The squall lasted for several more minutes, then finally died. The boat came back up into trim and we sailed on under reduced sails. During that squall with all the water splashing in the cockpit we lost about twenty of our favorite cassette tapes of classical music as well as the tape recorder and the ear phones. Well back to Radio Shack!

Six months before we went into the port of Aden, South Yemen had a civil war. One communist faction was fighting another one and the whole town was a pile of rubble. Also the harbor was dotted with the hulks of ships that had been sunk by cannon fire. As it was night when we entered, we couldn't see the hulks so called the Aden Pilots. They came out in a small boat and guided us around all dangers and to the anchorage at Steamer Point. We were only about 30 yards off the jetty and had a complete view of the ruined village.

Except for the immigration inspector, all of the authorities were user friendly. We decided that the immigration inspector took a Mean and Nasty pill every morning. No one can have that miserable a disposition without great effort.

There are no American authorities in Aden so we went to the British Embassy to get information about having money sent to us. We hadn't been able to use our credit cards since Bombay and that was a problem. Had those cards been issued on a Hong Kong bank they'd have been accepted. But that ruled out San Diego Trust and Savings.

So once more we contacted our trust officer and had her wire some more money to us. This time because of damage done by the civil war, I had to walk six kilometers to where I could make the telephone call to San Diego. Rarely could you find a taxi. Mostly we traveled by bus. In the meantime we took advantage of the great hospitality offered by the British. They took us all over the territory where non-Yemenis were allowed to travel and spent many delightful hours in their company.

At their suggestion we went to the supermarket near the foreign embassies. The doors were locked at 10:00 A.M. so you had to be in by then or no shopping. What was interesting was watching bus loads of Russian women arriving and buying cases of French wines being paid for with American dollars. There were about 50,000 Russians there and many families. Only American dollars, Swiss francs, or German marks were accepted for purchases; the Russians seemed to prefer American money.

After about one week I would go to the bank each day to see if our money arrived. The answer was always "No," so we settled in for a longer stay. We'd been given a 30-day visa when we entered and expected to use all of it.

In the harbor we were surrounded by dozens of eastern bloc freighters waiting to be refueled. Aden is a VERY busy harbor. Some years back Aden was considered the third busiest port in the world. Also nearby were two Russian naval vessels. One was a hospital ship and the other appeared to be a helicopter carrier. Each morning armed soldiers would do exercises on the flight deck of the carrier. We watched with great interest.

As we were anchored so close to the jetty, all of the small boats carrying Russian seamen ashore had to pass close by our stern. So we put up the largest American flag we had (4 x 6') and flew it proudly from our back stay. As the boats would go by we would wave at all the seamen. The younger ones would wave back, but the Stalin-age ones would look straight ahead and not acknowledge us. The same thing happened when we met them on the streets in town.

On the 23rd day of our stay, the Immigration officer stopped me as I went by his office on the way back from the bank. He said we would have to leave this very day. I told him we couldn't for our money wasn't in. "Oh, yes it is," the officer replied. "Go back to the bank and get it and leave."

I returned to the bank and sure enough my money was there. We refueled, topped off the water, and left. It seemed that they didn't like our flag. Tough!

It wasn't too far to the Straits of Bab el Mandeb leading into the Red Sea, but the big boat traffic got heavier. The Straits are quite narrow and off to the east is the island of Perim occupied by Russia. The charts all warn about getting within two miles for the Russians have artillery and gunboats stationed there and they do shoot if you get within their range. It was a bright sunny day as we started through and we stared at the island with concern. Especially as the big boats were coming closer and pushing us towards the island. We hoped the gunners on Perim could see two white-haired old people aboard the boat and know we were harmless. At least they didn't fire at us. We had a nice beam reach and went through the Straits at about five knots in the company of several freighters.

Before entering the Red Sea Janet had taken the charts and, with calipers, had measured off 35 miles from all Ethiopian territory. The Ethiopian pirates were well known and we wanted to stay well to the east of their country. In talking to people later we learned that no matter how far out we were the pirates would come after us if they wanted us. Still, we stayed on the eastern side of the Red Sea.

While the wind was mostly on our nose, we did make some northern progress. Slow, but steady. Several times we had to turn on the diesel, but we'd have done that anyway to charge the batteries. Also we had to have motor power to dodge the big boats. Some came awfully close.

Almost in the middle of the Red Sea, at the southern end, is an island named Jabal at Tair. At that time (1987) it belonged to North Yemen. The two Yemenis (North and South) have since merged and are now one country, but then it was a new country to us. The island is just the top of an old volcano and has just one anchorage on the southeast corner. We were tired of having to tack back and forth across the wind and decided to go into the anchorage for a rest.

As we motored in (very slowly) we saw two HUGE open boats dragged up on the shore and lots of men walking and sitting around. The ancient lava overhangs the shore and the whole thing looks like a giant cave. We could see that the men were washing their clothes and bathing. We waved at them and they waved back as they climbed back into their boats and left. They disappeared around the island and we have no idea where they were going. For there were no houses on the island and no fresh water. Was a mystery.

After three days we upped anchor once more and headed for Port Sudan on the west side of the Red Sea. After passing the north of the Ethiopian border, we turned directly toward Port Sudan. The channel was well marked but so many boats were wrecked upon the outer reefs that we were doubly cautious as we motored well into the harbor. The designated anchorage was behind a huge derelict boat and we found several other boats anchored there. It was a very congenial gathering and we enjoyed our short stay there. Checking in with the officials was probably the hardest of any county because of the language barrier and the various officials were in different parts of the town.

It was Ramadan, the Muslim month of fasting, and we found it interesting to see all the males drop to their knees and touch their foreheads to the ground five times during the day when the call came from the minaret. The women didn't seem to take part.

There was a superior open market in the town and that was about all. There were many fabric shops and a lot of sewing machines set up on the sidewalks. All were being operated by men.

And it was in that open market that we first tasted those delicious dark green melons from the Nile Valley. They were very small, about the size of a baseball, with thin skin and incredibly good flavor. We bought all that we could and loved every bite.

As Sudan is now Communist, we had to go through armed guards each time we went ashore. The young soldier would frisk me and then go through Janet's purse. She finally asked him what he was looking for. He replied, "Huh?" He had no idea what he was looking for; he had just been told to search all purses.

Port Sudan had many foreign makes of cars and trucks. They also had many big wagons and carts that required the motor power of a small donkey or ass, as they are known there. Most of the asses were only waist tall. A single ass would be hitched to a large wagon piled high with vegetables, fruits or freight. Sometimes the weight would be so heavy the poor animal would be unable to pull the wagon without help. This usually came from the crack of cruel whip or long rod of bamboo. I told Janet that if the good Lord decides to bring me back on this earth when I die, that I hope He will not reincarnate me as an ass in the Arab world.

Water was in great demand and there seemed to be a great

scarcity throughout Port Sudan. There were faucets almost all over town, but they were for bathing or washing clothes only. You would see people standing in line to take a quick bath. For drinking water, there was one faucet down by the water front, where even longer lines of people lined up with jerry jugs. Young boys or girls with a five gallon jug would have to manhandle it to wherever their home was. That is where we had to line up and wait for hours to fill several five gallon jugs for our boat. There was a fee for the water but I don't remember how much.

We were able to get diesel fuel from a large freighter out of Galveston, Texas, who was off loading wheat. We had to go alongside the freighter while they sent hoses over fifty feet long to siphon from the barrels they had on deck. It was a messy job, and I would only recommend fueling like that only in emergencies.

We stayed just 10 days in Port Sudan and then entered the Red Sea again. We tacked across the sea and again went up the east side. One reason is that we wanted to go the same direction as the big boats. Those going north are supposed to go up the Saudi side of the sea. However there were those free thinkers who go their own way. That's a bit alarming when you meet them where they're not supposed to be.

We didn't stop at any of the many tourist spots along the Egyptian coast. Frankly we were sick of the Red Sea and wanted to get into the Mediterranean as quickly as possible. And the farther north we went, the heavier the big boat traffic became.

Once we went through the Straits of Gubal and into the narrow Gulf of Suez we not only had to cope with the big boats, but there were oil rigs all over the east side of the Gulf and small boats were going back and forth across our bow. Add to that a fierce current and wind on our bow. With our diesel going at full bore, we were making just 1 knot per hour. In other words, we were almost standing still.

Because of the heavy boat traffic, we didn't dare try to tack across the Gulf. We motored all night long, burning fuel like crazy. At daybreak we could see that the Gulf had widened a little and we tacked back and forth across the shipping lanes. This can be suicidal if you don't keep a good watch, so we watched and did make some forward progress. When tacking over close to the Sinai Peninsula, we could understand why the children of Israel got angry with Moses. It was the most desolate country we have ever seen. The scenery looked like something by Dali, and having to spend 40 years there would be extremely difficult.

Tacking back toward the mainland of Egypt, I reminded Janet that we were very low on fuel and asked her to see if she could contact any of the supply boats that we had read about. She called on Channel 16 and a voice told her to stay on that frequency and call for "Marine Logistics".

She did and "Marine Logistics" answered and asked about our problem. She told them that we had little fuel left and not enough to reach the Suez Canal. We gave them our course, position, and speed, and they told us to stay on that course and in about one hour a boat named *Maradive IV* would come alongside. In exactly one hour, a beautiful 110-foot long boat came toward us. They asked if we had enough fuel to follow them for eight miles. I told them that I thought so, but we would keep our sails up just in case.

They led us into Marsa Zaytiyah, a bay we never could've found alone, for the sand haze covered it. The big boat anchored and told us to come along side and tie up. Janet was at the wheel and she heard me ask the price of their fuel. Then she heard me say, "My Gawd!" Certain that they wanted an exorbitant amount for the fuel she joined me in astonishment when I told her the fuel was free. No charge at all.

As our tanks and jerry jugs were being filled with fuel and water, the captain of the *Maradive IV* leaned over the railing and asked about our stores. Janet said they were okay but she could use some staples like flour, bread and eggs. Then the captain invited us aboard for dinner while the refueling was going on.

While biting into a delicious steak dinner, Janet noticed the cook pulling things from the freezer. On the counter was piled one half of a frozen lamb, about one dozen frozen chickens, and from the refrigerator were ten dozen eggs. Janet said,"Oh, you're supplying another boat."

The cook said, "No, Madam, this is for you." At Janet's shriek of dismay the cook asked "Don't you like our food?" She assured him that we did, but we had just a small freezer and refrigerator and no room to store all he intended to give to us.

The captain laughed and told Janet not to worry and that the crew would take care of us while we finished dinner. When we returned to our boat we were struck dumb over the bounty that we found on board. Our cockpit, galley cutting board and counters, the dinette table, and the settee were filled with boxes of food. And it was all free.

There were chickens, eggs (about 4 dozen), potatoes, pita bread, honey, every fresh fruit and vegetable imaginable and all sorts of canned goods. There was even a can of that favorite Arabic candy, halvah. We're not certain, but we feel that because we didn't ask for much, we were given a lot. Perhaps if you went hog wild and asked for the world, they wouldn't be so generous. At any rate we discovered that the man who owns Maradive Oil Company is a sailor and he once ran into trouble and someone helped him. So he promised himself that if he ever had enough money he would help other people. There are 15 Maradive boats and 13 of them are always on duty in the Gulf of Suez while 2 are taking leave in Alexandria. The crews of the boats are former Egyptian Navy officers and seamen and are extremely polite and capable. They informed us that they would help any boat in trouble, no matter what flag it flew.

As we were having trouble with our SATNAV, they towed us to a mooring buoy and then put two electrical engineers on board to help us. A gale was blowing up, and our boat was really bouncing around, which made working difficult, but the engineers fixed our SATNAV (using some of their spare parts) and returned to their boat. The *Maradive IV* left the following morning as they had to go to the aid of another boat.

The winds were so severe that we decided to stay where we were for a while. Also in the harbor was a large freighter that acted as a supply boat for a French oil company. The deck was covered with pipes, drill bits, and such equipment. At that time the crew were Egyptians. They took turns each three months with a Filipino crew. But each day the Egyptian captain would zip over in his huge inflatable and say, "Come to dinner, do your laundry, eat ice cream, and see a movie!" His name was Magdi and he was a delight.

I may have saved the job of a captain on a large freighter. The freighter had been anchored about 200 yards off our starboard beam but now his anchor was dragging and it was about to go aground. The wind was blowing fiercely when I spotted the freighter apparently out of control and dragging his anchor. I made several calls on the VHF radio, and soon there was a lot of activity aboard the freighter as well as several vessels coming to the rescue. Fortunately the freighter was able to retrieve his anchor and motor to a safe spot for reanchoring. Otherwise it was a very ho-hum, but very windy day.

We stayed 10 days in that location with the winds blowing fiercely until I couldn't stand it any more. I said, "One more day of this wind and I'll go absolutely stark raving mad." So we made plans to leave the following morning, no matter what the weather. Then another Maradive boat, Number X, came in and called us on the radio. They asked were we okay and did we need some more stores and to come to dinner. We motored over and tied alongside them and sat down to another delicious dinner. When we returned to our boat, we found that they'd done the same thing to us as before. Every bare space was covered with boxes of food. We had enough for an army. We tied to another mooring buoy for the night as it took most of the afternoon to stow all our new provisions.

We left the harbor early the next morning. The sky was clear and bright and once outside the harbor of Marsa Zaytiyah there was very little wind. So we motored north to Port Tewfik at the southern end of the Suez Canal.

You must have an agent to take care of all your paperwork when going through the canal. We had been advised to use "The Prince of The Red Sea" on VHF Channel 16. Within a short time his representative stepped aboard and guided us to the small anchorage in front of the Port Tewfik Yacht Club. There we anchored and prepared to enjoy our stay. The Prince's sons and his representatives were marvelous people. They invited us to dinner and took us to barbecues and drove us all around.

They arranged special hotel accommodations for us in Cairo and the youngest son, Shemi, was our chauffeur for the week we were being tourists in his home town. We think we saw everything and enjoyed it all, especially the visit in the Prince's home and getting to meet the rest of his family.

Shemi took us to an authentic Egyptian restaurant for dinner one night. Only Egyptians patronized the place. The food, needless to say, was a little strange for our American taste, but nevertheless delicious and we enjoyed every bite. Before the dinner, Janet wanted to wash her hands as she had been riding "Honey," a camel at the Pyramids. Janet went into the ladies' room, but couldn't find any paper to dry her hands. With dripping hands and a little exasperated, she came out the door to find a four year old boy holding a roll of paper towels, with his right hand out saying, "*Baksheesh, Baksheesh.*" Children learn the value of money very early in life in the Arab world.

We paid the required fees and readied ourselves for the passage up the canal. It's a two day trip and we were anxious to get it over with. Our pilot was scheduled to arrive at 2:00 AM, but he didn't show up until 3:00 AM. We viewed this as ominous. This fear was borne out when he arrived pounding on his chest and saying that he was Number One. He guided our boat around the sand bars at the end of the canal and then began making demands. He wanted whiskey, beer, cigarettes, shirts, and hats. I gave him a hat and nothing else. He gave a few Arabic shouts and continued to steer the boat. He was also a good helmsman.

At that time we were terribly under-propellered and were not making too much speed. Number One complained bitterly and kept trying to turn the engine up. I had to tell him that the engine would burn out if he did that, and the next time he touched the accelerator except to slow down I would cut him off at the knees. I think he took my threat seriously as I appeared very angry. So Number One just grumbled and reluctantly left the engine alone. Then he spied my knife on the coach roof and wanted it. Janet took it below out of temptation's way. She also served him two meals and several snacks and he never once said "Thank you". Number One was a pain.

We sighted the port of Ismailia with great relief. Here we would get rid of our arrogant pilot and spend the night. Number One directed us in front of a large freighter and told us to anchor there. I argued with him that when we backed down to set the anchor we would be too close to the big boat. "Drop the anchor now!" shouted Number One, so I did reluctantly.

Before heading up the canal, we had been told never to tip the pilots more than $5.00US, and that's what Janet handed to that nasty pilot. He looked at the bill in his hand, sneered and said, "Is that all?" Janet reached out to take it away and he closed his fingers over it and cut loose with a spate of Arabic. We felt he was not wishing us a good day. Then he climbed over the side and disappeared aboard the waiting pilot boat. Thank heavens!

When we had backed down to set the anchor, we were much too close to the big boat and we had to move. So much for Number One's seamanship in anchoring. Safely anchored away from all vessels, we ate dinner and went to bed. It had been a very nerve-wracking, exhausting day.

Our next pilot was due to arrive at 6:00 AM but didn't show up until 8:00 AM, and what a nice surprise he was. A very pleasant older man, he had none of the arrogance and braggadocio of our first escort and brought with him some fresh fruit, tomatoes and hot rolls. It was a great beginning.

Our new pilot turned out to be very capable at the wheel, so we relaxed and let him take over. There certainly isn't much to see along the shores of the Suez except for the burned out remnants of several wars. The canal is pretty if you like the color brown, for that's all the color there is. Which could explain why you never see any pictures of it.

After another long day, we reached Port Said and said goodbye to our second pilot. He advised us to go to the Port Said Yacht Club to spend the night, but we had heard through the cruising grapevine that the facilities were very poor, expensive, and dirty, so we elected to go on and leave Egypt. It is impossible to explain the feeling we had when we passed the end of the breakwaters marking the beginning of the Suez Canal and knew that we were at last in the Mediterranean.

CHAPTER SEVEN

Once past all the freighters and military vessels waiting to begin the southward passage through the Suez Canal, we went out farther for about ten miles. Then we made one of the smartest moves we've ever made–we turned right towards Tel Aviv, Israel.

In case you don't already know it, you can't find any charts for Israel. A friend in Galle, Sri Lanka, had told us, with a smile, "Don't worry about it, the Israelis will find you." So all through the night we sailed east with light winds.

On the VHF radio we heard many of the big boats putting out calls for "Israeli Navy, Israeli Navy". Then they'd give their boat name, country of origin, cargo, number of crew, last port of call and the port they were heading. The Israeli Navy would answer them and give them an okay to proceed. We thought that was a great idea so began calling the Israeli Navy. They never answered, but we kept on going.

While fixing breakfast the following morning Janet heard me say "We've got company!" Circling our boat was a small plane. It circled about three times and then headed for shore. Janet was below dishing up breakfast when the roar of jet planes brought her up on deck. Two Israeli jet fighters streaked over the boat, not too far above the top of the mast. They flew out for several miles and then back again. Clearly visible beneath their wings were armed rockets. The Israelis are always prepared. When the planes left I said, "Well Janet, they know we're here."

Janet dashed below and finished up the breakfast dishes when I called, "And here they come!" Zooming toward us was an Israeli gunboat. It was moving at an incredible speed and making very little sound. About 50 feet from us it came about, and facing us were three 20mm cannon, one on the bow, one on the stern and one on the cabin roof. Three young Israelis were manning them and no one was smiling. "Janet would you take the wheel for a minute please?" I went to the side of the cockpit, put my hands in the air, and said, "Don't shoot fellas, we're friendlies." They just looked at me with no expression and still not smiling. Then a voice called to us over the loudspeaker and asked who we were and what were we doing in Israeli waters. We gave our names and said that we wanted to visit Israel as tourists. They asked our country of origin although they could see our American flag. We learned later that they were listening for accents, probably something Arabic. We gave them all the information asked of us, mainly how many were aboard our boat. When the questions ended, we were told to stay in the cockpit where they could see us, not to change course or speed and that a police boat was on it's way out to us. Although they still trained their 20mm canon on us, we felt no apprehension. The Israelis are well trained in gunnery.

When the police boat arrived, a man in civilian clothes and with a revolver in his hand came on board and apologized to us for the inconvenience and said he would have to go below and look around. After a short time he came out into the cockpit and spoke, in Hebrew, to the gunboat over a handheld VHF radio. Then he started laughing. The gunboat cannons were secured, the men smiled at us for the first time, and the gunboat sped away. Janet asked the policeman what that was all about. He said that he informed the gunboat that there were no terrorists or munitions down below and he felt they needn't worry for the woman was putting up a mezzuzah, but was putting it up backwards.

That needs some explanation we're sure. When we were getting ready to launch our boat, some Jewish friends had asked what we wanted as a christening gift for the boat. We said a mezzuzah. All Jewish homes have one attached to each window and door. On the outside of the small container is a plaque that says, in Hebrew, "God's blessing on all who enter here." Inside the mezzuzah is a rolled piece of papyrus that is covered with more prayers. We had placed that mezzuzah on our main hatch but felt it prudent to remove it when entering Arab territory, just in case. Now Janet was replacing it, backwards. The policeman took it from her, placed his hand over his head in place of the traditional yarmulke, said a few prayers and our mezzuzah was back where it belonged.

We asked the policeman to stay aboard our boat and enter Tel Aviv harbor with us. He agreed and did just that. He and his family became such good friends to us and we'll always be grateful to them for the things they did for us.

It was necessary for me to return to San Diego for some surgery so it was decided that Janet would stay with the boat in Israel during my absence. I caught a military Space A flight out of Ben Gurion Airport in Israel and headed back to the States. During the three months that I was gone, Janet said she never felt so well cared for in all her life. Every day at least a dozen people would knock on the hull and ask if she was okay, did she need anything, or issue an invitation. She was invited into private homes for all of the holiday celebrations and for Sabbath suppers. It was a tremendous experience for her and she couldn't have been in better hands.

Before I left for the States, our policeman friend had driven us all over Israel. We'd gone as far north as the Lebanese border and then down through the Israel Valley, but we hadn't gone to Jerusalem. And that was first on our list of things we had to see.

One day Janet was sitting in the cockpit when she heard a voice say, "Hello, are you really from San Diego?" She could see a man standing there with two teenaged girls, his nieces it turned out. Janet asked him aboard and it was another of those wonderful things that we seem to be so fortunate to have happen to us. My comment: Janet never met a stranger, no matter what creed, color, religion, or race they were, they were always treated with utmost respect and courtesy. Janet always said of me, that I always greet a person with a hearty handshake.

The man's name was Aaron. He was a graduate of Columbia University and had directed many TV shows in the States. He returned to Israel to fight in their wars and founded the TV industry in Israel. It ran in his family for his father was the founder of the Israeli movie business. Anyway, he asked Janet what our plans were when I returned to Tel Aviv. She told him that we wanted to visit all the Christian sights in and around Jerusalem and in other places where it was safe to visit. He told her to call him before we went to Jerusalem and she replied that we'd call him after we were settled there. He said, "You're not going to settle anywhere, you're going to stay with me in my home."

What he had forgotten to tell us was that for twenty years he had been an amateur archaeologist in Jerusalem. So for the five days we stayed with him we were taken over, under, through, on top of, and around Jerusalem. He narrated each archeological site. biblical history etc., until we felt we were a part of it and now began to understand a little of the history of the Jewish race. Many times I had read the Bible, not understanding a tenth of what I had read. With Aaron's background, experience, education, and explanations, we now understood and we saw things that the average tourist never sees or hears. We are so grateful for that experience.

One that will always live in our minds was the swearing in ceremony for the newly inducted soldiers into the Israeli army. It was by torchlight and was held at the Wailing Wall. There were dozens of soldiers standing atop the surrounding wall looking out with their weapons ready for any emergency. The year before a terrorist had thrown a grenade over the wall into the crowd at the ceremony and many people had been killed. The whole ceremony was very impressive.

That same evening we had another impressive experience. Our friend drove us to the Mount of Olives and parked. The moon was full, and we stared across the Garden of Gethsemane and looked at the old walled city of Jerusalem. Our eyes filled with tears.

They filled again as we went to see Yad Vashem, the Museum of the Holocaust. We defy anyone to see that with dry eyes. It is awe inspiring.

We were also taken to all the battle sites in Jerusalem, Ammunition Hill, and the old City itself. We found it so incredible that such a small number of defiant Israelis could hold off thousands of enemies who wanted to kill them. Being a retired U.S. Marine and having fought in three campaigns in the Pacific during World War II, I was highly impressed by their strategy, bravery, resourcefulness, and cunning. The battle of Ammunition Hill was a most fierce battle. A Company of Israeli soldiers was trying to take Ammunition Hill occupied by 3000 Arabs. All the Israeli officers were killed in the first few minutes of battle. Most of the enlisted personnel also were killed and a few retreated. But three young Israeli soldiers didn't get the word to retreat. The three, by their sheer courage, fought like possessed demons and routed the entire Arab force. Of the three young soldiers one was wounded in the leg by a stray bullet. They were decorated with the highest medals.

One of the most impressive things about Israel is their archeological digs. Space in Israel is very limited. Rather than disturb thousands of years of culture, buildings are built atop the digs, so they enjoy the best of two cultures, the very old and up to recent times.

When we returned to Tel Aviv we made preparations to leave Israel. We had to stop in Haifa first. In the States I had purchased a computer and brought it all the way back from San Diego. I left it with customs in Haifa rather than pay a huge import fee and tax, so now that we were leaving Israel we had to pick it up.

While touring around Jerusalem we had met a very nice young couple from Haifa who stayed with us to listen to Aaron tell what we were seeing. This couple invited us to call them when we reached Haifa and they were our hosts for the week we were there.

The husband was the manager of the only automobile production plant in Israel and gave us a grand tour of it. They also manufactured the vehicles for the Israeli Army, designed with armor plating underneath to protect occupants against mines. A very efficient operation.

Our hostess drove us to Nazareth to see the home of St. Mary and other Christian sites there. There was a very beautiful church there. Nations of the world had been invited to place art work depicting the "Madonna and Child" on a given space inside the church. All were different and beautifully done with mosaics, except that of the United States. Now please don't take me wrong. To many, modern art, I'm sure, is beautiful. I do not like modern art. I personally did not like the United States art work in this church. I thought it sacrilege to place modernistic artwork like this in a house of worship. I'm sorry, just call me an old man–confused, bewildered, and an old fogy. When I see art work I want to be able to immediately know that it is, without having to guess what the artist had in his mind.

We stayed in Haifa several days, enjoying the company of our host and hostess. For a quick meal one evening we went to the Golden Arches and yes, we enjoyed not a "Big Mac," but a "McDavid".

For another evening repast, we enjoyed a very international meal cooked by two wonderful ladies, our beautiful Jewish hostess and my very charming American wife. The meal–Oh Yes! Italian spaghetti.

We badly wanted to go south to Bethlehem and Massada, but the PLO were rattling their swords and those spots were off limits. So we picked up our computer and, under the eyes of the Customs officer, we left the yacht harbor, waving goodbye to our gracious hostess.

The overnight sail to Larnaca, Cyprus, was uneventful. Months earlier we had written for a mooring reservation in the Larnaca Marina so we went right in to the harbor and tied to the guest dock. We were assigned a berth and settled in for a three year stay–at least in the winters, we were cruising each summer.

The ambience in Larnaca Marina was glorious. Also it's location was so convenient. You just had to go out the gates and the city was right there. Cyprus is a diamond of an island and Larnaca it's perfect setting.

All winter long there were barbecues at the marina each weekend. As there were many people aboard boats spending each winter, there was always a good turn out. And for three New Year's Eve parties several of us staged a roasted pig dinner.

The pig weighed about 100 pounds and all the attending men took turns for an hour of turning the pig on a spit and basting it. Janet was in charge of preparing the stuffing and that was quite a job.

Boats, as a rule, have small ranges in their gallies, so Janet had to parcel out the loaves of bread to be dried in ovens. Many boats along each dock had first mates who were busy cubing slices of bread and putting them in their ovens. Then Janet took them, mixed in spices, onions, and the like and turned the whole thing over to me to stuff in the pig sew it up and supervise the men turning the spit for about twelve hours.

The first time we did this, it was quite an amateurish job and we learned from that experience. The pig was burned a little but still was delicious.

The next year it was more professional, in that we had the marina maintenance shop build a much stronger barbecue and spit. After all, these pigs run almost 100 pounds each. Then my friend Manny took an old washing machine motor and by some clever reconstruction made a motorized spit. This eased the operation considerably and when the pig was cut up for eating was the best I've ever eaten.

Our summers in the Eastern Mediterranean were spent cruising Turkey, Greece, and the Greek Islands. One summer we were invited by Brit friends John and Joan to go on their 46 foot power boat to cruise the Turkish coast. We entered Turkey at the port of Fenike and cruised all the way up the coast (1,000 plus miles) to Istanbul and have nothing but praise for Turkey. The coast line is spectacular and with history at every inch. From the sea we could see villages that hadn't been occupied for hundreds of years, but the paths were still visible and the orchards still producing. Most of them could be entered only from the sea as there were no roads.

One afternoon we anchored behind an island that was covered with the ruins of a village that once must have held at least 50,000 people. Now the village was empty and in ruins. There were ruins of two Christian churches so it predated the Ottoman Empire. And unfortunately the Turks don't delve into the history of anything that happened before they arrived. So no one knows who these island people were, where they came from, or what happened to them. The Turkish government is most reluctant to issue permits for archaeologists to dig into their history. And that's a shame.

One of the most spectacular sights along the Turkish coast is Kekova Roads. Sailing along before you enter the pass into the harbor, you see ahead in the water what look like rocks sticking up. But, when you get closer, you can see that they are steps leading nowhere. In the clear water you can see the ruins of houses below you. You are literally sailing through their dining rooms, while on the hill stands a ruined crenellated castle. It seems that the castle and the village were destroyed in an earthquake that occurred 2500 years before. There are many sarcophagi around, some in the water, but who were these people? We'll probably never know.

Another good thing about cruising in Turkish waters, in addition to the scenery and the people, is the superb Turkish bread. It must be the best we have ever tasted and is available in all the villages where we stopped. Baked fresh every morning, the long loaves are truly a taste delight. John, our captain, was the "sniffer outer" and for exercise would scout out this marvelous bread and bring it to the boat so hot he had to juggle to carry it. John and I used to fight over who got the heel end of the loaf as it was so desirable.

John was one of the greatest delegators I have ever known. He would say, "Frank, the anchor windlass is down, do you think you could repair it?" I had so many little repair jobs going that it took most of my time, cannibalizing old pumps, windlasses, stereos etc., that I seemed to be busy all the time doing maintenance work. Joan thought I could repair anything.

When we entered Kusadasi, Turkey, John met a Turkish friend of his who owned a sixty-foot very expensive power boat. Unfortunately, his friend had been harbor bound for several days because his microwave oven was down. They couldn't find a repairman to fix it. Joan was saying, "I'll check with Frank, I'll bet he can fix it." Thank you very much, Joan, for your trust in me, but I know from nothing about microwaves.

It was here that John mentioned to me that he had only asked Janet and I along on the trip as far as Istanbul, but that we had worked out quite well as crew members and would we like to go on to Athens, Greece, with them. Without hesitation I accepted his offer if he raised our salaries. He quipped back that immediately he would double our salaries. Double times zero is not much increase.

After many weeks of cruising northward, we finally went through the Dardanelles and into the Sea of Marmara. With Europe on one side and Asia on the other, this sea is another treasure trove of history. Vast fleets of ships from many of the ancient Mediterranean countries lie on the bottom of the sea. Remnants of long ago wars.

We stopped at Port Marmara on the island of Marmara and spent two pleasant days there. The harbor and the small village were very crowded for it was a Turkish religious holiday. But we enjoyed excellent meals at local restaurants and loaves of their wonderful bread. Then it was on to Istanbul.

The Atakoy Marina on the north coast was to be our home for the next six weeks. John and Joan had to fly back to England for about a month. Their power boat was ours to invite our friends and we did. The marina is massive and had just recently opened when we were there. They had won many prizes for excellence and, in our opinion, should give them all back for it was the most poorly designed and planned facility we had ever seen. That was in 1988 and perhaps things have changed since then, but it's doubtful. There was just one set of toilets and with many boats at least 1/2 mile away they were most inconvenient. And you were forbidden to use the heads on your boat. Just think of it, "The Sultan's revenge at 2:30 A.M." and half a mile from the nearest toilet.

Another failing was that the water was undrinkable so you had to buy jugs of bottled water from a truck that came by each day. But you could buy bags of ice cubes from the marina, and guess what water was used to make them. Yep!, the undrinkable stuff. But the security was great. There was one security guard

for every seven boats and they were all very pleasant men.
And we did love Istanbul. It and Jerusalem are the most interesting and exciting cities we have seen. The old walled city to the west of the Golden Horn was especially attractive to us. Full of narrow streets, tiny shops and excellent cafes, we spent many happy days there. And the Egyptian Spice Market was another great draw.

The world's finest museum is Topkapi Palace and is a must for any Istanbul visitor. Impossible to describe for it is chock full of magnificent treasures with the Sultan's Harem being the first thing you must see. It's an all day trip so plan for it and don't worry about taking a sandwich, for they have an excellent restaurant.

Then there are the Blue Mosque and Sancta Sophia which are breath-taking. And something else worth seeing are Justinian's Cisterns which are underground. All that water enabled the Turks to withstand so many years of sieges. They believed in being prepared.

There is so much to see and do in Istanbul that it's impossible to list all the activities, but one thing bears repeating, and remember that word "bear." We had left the Egyptian Spice Market and walked across the street to a small cafe for some kebabs which, like all Turkish food, were delicious. Upon leaving the cafe Janet was in the lead when something brushed against her leg. She looked down and saw a huge golden bear gallumphing down the street. He was wearing no collar or muzzle and right behind him was another bear, his twin. About 10 feet behind them was a man carrying a stick and apparently their keeper. Janet was startled and she asked me, "What was that brushed against me?"

I replied, "I didn't see any bears."

Janet said, "Thank heaven, I thought I was losing my mind." Only in Istanbul.

When we left Istanbul we went east through the Bosporus. Many of the villages along the shores were centuries old, interspersed with modern structures. We went into the Black Sea just far enough to say that we'd been there, stick a toe in the water which was cold (and probably polluted), then turned around and went west again. We spent two nights anchored in the Prince's Islands and returned to Port Marmara for another night's stay. Our destination was now Cannakale for we wanted to take a tour of Troy.

We hired a taxi and had them drive us the few miles to the ancient site. The scenery along the way was so historical with the Gallipolis peninsula across the way and then we were at Troy.

Many people feel that the remains of that city are too small to be the same city as described by Homer in the *Iliad*, but we were impressed. The only thing that didn't impress us was the horrible big wooden horse at the entrance. Full of windows and German tourists (all shouting and taking pictures) it added nothing to the scene. But from the top of the slight hill we could look down on what had once been the bay at Troy, but was now silted over.

Janet's imagination went rampant. To no one in particular she said aloud. "Can't you imagine a troop of ancient soldiers marching with their swords and spears ready for battle? I can almost hear their bare feet slapping in the dust and the noise of their battle dress as they are trying to march quietly." We spent the entire day at Troy and returned to the boat exhausted but exhilarated.

I said, "I learned more and will remember more about ancient history in a few short weeks than I ever learned in school."

Once more we went into the Aegean Sea and headed toward the Northern Sporades Islands of Greece. There were several good anchorages on the way north to Kavala, Greece and we stopped each night. On the third day we entered the harbor at Kavala and prepared for a week's stay. It's a charming city with a great open market and excellent restaurants.

To put icing on the cake, some friends from Cyprus came in and tied to the dock a short distance from us. We were ever so glad to see them, as they loaned us heavy sweaters to wear on our way back to Cyprus. When we left Larnaca we had planned only to go as far as Istanbul. Now it was ending September and it was beginning to get cold. Our friend from Cyprus said to me one day, "Your boat, *The Isle of Barra,* it's named, I presume, after the Isle of Barra in Scotland. I have been there. The people there are sure strange."

Ready to defend my ancestral home, I said, "What do you mean strange?"

He replied, "Well sir, I was there, several times. I know the place. It's generally cold, windy, and rainy. No wonder the people are strange. One day I met a milk maid who said she had started milking her cows one hour earlier every day so that at the end of the month she could have a day off."

Our first stop on leaving Kavala was Port Thassos on the north side of the island of Thassos. A small comfortable harbor within walking distance of the village. We had a wonderful dinner at one of the harbor-side restaurants and sampled the delicious liqueur made only on that island. It is called "Amelia" and is made from walnuts and honey. I wanted to buy a case of it and discovered that there was only one bottle left on the whole island. So I bought it. It seems that it's seasonal and we were there at the end of the season.

Heading southwest, Mt. Olympus soon came into view. It is one of the sites used by ancient sailors to find their way home. It was clearly visible at the southern end of the peninsula as were the many monasteries along its sides. All females were verboten on those premises, but we read that they were now allowing in hens to get fresh eggs. Accessible only by water, we couldn't see how any boat could moor alongside the rock piers. The swells had built to about 20 feet and the passage was very rough. We did pull into two small ports for some rest from the seas and wind. Then it was on to Skopelos.

CHAPTER EIGHT

The islands around Skopelos were charming. We went into many delightful anchorages and returned to Skopelos three times. That island had a safe, sheltered harbor with excellent restaurants along the waterfront. As usual, we did some shopping there before we had to leave, heading west again.

We stopped in one port for the night and then went through the channel between the Greek mainland and the island of Evvoia. The scenery was green and beautiful and we tried to imagine all of the battles that had been fought on this land.

We tied to a dock in the city of Khalkis and went across the bridge to let the harbormaster know that we were there and wanted to go through the bridge. We were told to be ready to motor through at 2:00 AM when the lights came on and the bells rang. But that didn't happen until an hour later than scheduled. Finally the lights came on and the bells rang. The bridge parted in the middle and telescoped straight back toward the banks. That was the only bridge I have ever witnessed that telescoped like that. Then we motored through, tied to another dock, and tried to sleep for the rest of the night. It was very hot inside our staterooms so we didn't sleep hardly at all. We had been told that there were hundreds of rats roaming around at night. We closed the boat as much as possible–we sure didn't want any pests aboard. I didn't see any rats but I suppose they were out there.

We had planned to go many miles the next day, but a gale blew in and we had to pull into a small port on Evvoia to ride it out. The next day we headed south again to round Cape Sounion. That was a two day trip and we were glad to see the Temple of Apollo on the top of the cape. From the sea it looked (through binoculars) like it had been a beautiful structure in those ancient days. Now all we saw were tall columns or pillars still standing.

This was the second familiar sight that ancient sailors looked for. The temple is 4500 years old and from the sea looked beautiful. Following the ancient tradition of making a toast to Poseidon, I poured a bottle of Greek wine into the sea. This is supposed to insure good weather on to Athens. The bottle of wine must have been an off brand and none of us could drink it. Apparently Poseidon didn't like our offering either for we were soon in the midst of another gale. As this was summer, all of the marinas were full so we headed for Piraeus and the very expensive Zea Marina. There we stayed for three days before leaving for Cyprus. We thanked John and Joan for a wonderful cruise and bid them a tearful goodbye. John was selling his boat here in Athens area to get a larger boat. (And one I hoped that required less maintenance to keep it in Bristol Fashion).

I booked Janet's and my return trip to Cyprus on a "Love Boat," a cruise liner that would take us back via Rhodes and then on to Cyprus. We had a small cubicle of a cabin with private shower. It was hardly big enough to turn around, but it was adequate and that was all that mattered. Having been in Cyprus for over a year we had became acquainted with many people and guess who?–a lovely couple that we had been associating with, attended many of their parties, and stayed in their home a couple of times. It was like old home week and it was a very pleasurable trip back to Cyprus.

There was never a dull moment in Cyprus. In the winter time you could find about 65 British citizens, 20-30 Germans, Dutch, Danish and Scandinavians, sometimes as many as 15 to 18 Americans and Canadians, a smattering of French, Australian, South African, Italian and of course many Cypriot fishermen. A very international community. Besides the weekly BBQ's, dances, and parties, there was skiing in the mountains, gliders at the British air base, and other hobbies, such as hiking, photography, etc. There were many fine restaurants, most with very modest prices, which Janet and I frequented often. But twice a week about thirty or forty of us got together for bridge lessons on Monday and duplicate bridge on Thursday. Before we took the lessons, Janet and I took first prize in the bridge tournament. The second year, after we became schooled in the game, we turned out in about 18th place. You'd think we would get smarter. My conclusion is that I guess ignorance truly is bliss. Apparently we were slower learners than the other people.

We have made many life time friends from that little community and we communicate often by various media, snail mail correspondence, radio, telephone, and the latest by electronic e-mail emissions.

From the hundred plus boats in Cyprus there were several children, probably 35 to 40 in number. Most of them were very well mannered and a delight to have around, except at a BBQ where one little boy ate piece after piece of Janet's baklava. Janet told his mother, "Why don't you have your son eat something else, and save a few bits of baklava for the adults. Your boy doesn't know from baklava." By the way Janet was paid the highest of all compliments by a couple of Greek ladies when they asked for her recipe for baklava.

Getting back to the children, the majority of those sailing were going to the local schools or taking correspondence courses and being tutored by their parents. I have never seen such a bright, intelligent group of kids. Most, if enrolled in the U.S. school system, would be two or three grades higher than the regular classes.

One little girl in particular I really fell in love with. If it were possible I would have adopted her. But that happened in Tahiti. She was nine years old. She of course knew basic English. While in Africa she had learned the Africaans (Dutch) and the Swahili Bantu (tongue clicking) languages. Then her folks sailed to Venezuela where she readily picked up the Spanish language. Then the folks sailed on to French Polynesia where she learned Chinese, French, and Tahitian. She was fluent enough in all the languages and was the interpreter for her parents when there was a language barrier. The amazing thing about this little girl was you would have thought that she being so talented, and not the normal little girl, that she would have been a very sassy and precocious child. She did not have one bit of sassy precociousness about her at all. Her parents should have been very proud of her.

The other cruising we did in the Greek Islands was uneventful. But when we were leaving Cyprus forever, we went back to Mandraki Harbor on Rhodes for a few days. There were several old friends from Larnaca there and we enjoyed our stay. Then it was on to Simi and Procopi. Between those two islands my fishing reel started to sing. Janet yelled that I had a strike and I yelled back to her, "Let that sucker drown–I'm too busy taking down the sails." We were about to enter the port of Livadhi. Just then the fish jumped and a sword came out of the water. I had a swordfish! WOW! A small one, but still a swordfish. I reeled it in, gaffed it, and brought it aboard in the cockpit. I didn't really catch this fish, I stole it. The lure (hook) was caught in the swordfish bill. I still claim it. It was quite active flailing around, so I tied the bill and tail together encircling the binnacle, so it wouldn't goose Janet or the cat. I still had anchoring to do.

Our cat Tigger almost went wild. He wasn't just saying meow, but MEOW! You could have heard him across the bay. Then he would jump off the cockpit seat hit the fish between his eyes with his paw (POW-POW, take that you sucker, MEOW!) and jump back on the seat again. He repeated the process until I came back to the cockpit to clean the fish. Janet and I almost died laughing at him. The fish was delicious. Each of us got two nice sword fish steaks, including Tigger, who had really worked hard in subduing the fish. Our refrigeration was down so we donated about thirty steaks to the Greek Navy (one of their warships was anchored close by). I am sure the officers dined sumptuously in fine cuisine style.

Our next stop was Astipalaia and that was a costly mistake. A German sailor in the harbor at Simi had said that every time he thought about Astipalaia he thought about storms. We should've listened. The entrance to the main harbor on the south coast is studded with small islands and rocks and we had gale force winds again. The Aegean's *meltemi* had struck with force. We wanted to motor in, but the motor wouldn't start so we tried to make headway under storm sails. We were heeling far over when one of our sail bags rolled off the deck and over the side.

Janet brought the boat around and I tried to pick up the bag with a boat hook. Unfortunately I picked up the wrong end and the sail slipped out of the bag and down to the bottom of the sea. It was our best Genoa and wasn't cheap.

We finally entered the harbor under sail. The harbor was very crowded and we couldn't go in very far, so Janet brought the bow into the wind, and I dropped the anchor and lowered the sails. I wasn't at all happy about our position, but it was the best we could do under the circumstances. We ate dinner and even though it was very early we both were dead tired and went to bed.

A strange motion of the boat awakened me at about midnight. I went on deck and found that we had dragged anchor and were drifting towards some ominous lumps in the water. I yelled for Janet to take the helm and then I quickly raised the sails as she pointed the bow out into the open sea. Finally clear of dreadful Astipalaia, we now turned towards Anaphi Island.

Rod Heikel's "Cruising The Greek Waters" calls Anaphi a "great burned lump of an island" and that it may be, but the little bight on the southwestern corner sheltered us for three days while a Force 8 *meltemi* blew overhead.

It was here that Tigger, sitting close to me, anxiously awaited for me to catch a fish as the normal routine. I caught the small fish all right. Just as I was taking it off the hook, and Tigger batting at it with his paw, I felt excruciating pain in my right hand. "Janet, come here quick," I called. She told me that poison from the pectoral fins had penetrated my fingers and that I was due for about two hours of extreme pain. There wasn't much we could do for it except soak it in very hot water. Tigger was sulking and wouldn't have a thing to do with me until I picked up the pole again the following week.

Both of us wanted to visit Santorini, but that was not to be. Upon leaving Anaphi, the whole sky was hazy and the closer we got to Santorini the thicker the haze became. We anchored for the night on the south side of the island, which we could barely see.

The next morning the haze was even worse and as we were

going past the entrance to the main harbor a huge cruise ship pulled out, just barely visible. We decided it was much too dangerous to try and enter under those conditions so we turned south to Crete. Now the prevailing wind for Crete is the *meltemi* and it was really blowing. We wanted to enter the island at Khania, but the wind pushed us east to Rethminon. They really have no facilities for yachts so we had to tie to the same dock used by the cruise boats. It wasn't very comfortable so we left after two days.

We ventured into the super-secret port of Soudha, turned around, and left again. No one seemed to care about a little sail boat in their port as we were not challenged. We went a few miles north on the Akrotiri Peninsula and spotted a perfect anchorage on our port side. There were two houses on the hill overlooking it and a beach at the end. In 24 feet of water we dropped our hook. We stayed there for three days before leaving for Khania. It was a great gunkhole just to sit back and relax.

The port at Khania dates back to Venetian times and is truly historic and picturesque. Only one thing ruins it, the disco on the dock that is about 20 feet from your bow. It runs from 9:00 PM to 4:00 AM and the noise is at it's loudest. If we hear "These Boots Are Made For Walking" one more time we'll scream. Nancy you have a great voice but–over and over and over? We had to stay for a week as our generator was being repaired, so we had to listen to that.

The islands north of Crete offer little in the way of anchorages so we sailed straight through to the Peloponnesos peninsulas. These are really very nice places to visit. In one anchorage at the end of the Lakonikos Bay we stayed for ten days. We were secure and the little village provided everything we needed.

When we left we sailed around the southern tip of the next peninsula and into Messiniakos Bay and on to the port of Kalamata. This is a very pleasant town and we met some wonderful people there, which made it difficult to leave, but we did.

John Protopapas became our friend and mentor. He had lived in Canada for many years and could speak very good English. He told us that he was going to take us to a place for an authentic Greek meal. "You haven't tasted cuisine this good any place. The only thing is we will have to set up a table under a tree and carry out chairs and set the table. Then an old woman, eighty years of age, dressed in black with only one tooth in her head, who has prepared the food, will serve it when she is ready." John was right to every detail including the one tooth. This is what cruising is all about.

Before rounding the tip of the next peninsula we made several nice stops at small villages and islands. Then it was into Pilos Harbor. Following the advice of friends we went clear down to the northern end of the bay and dropped anchor in 15 feet of water above sand. It was good holding and we could see the ancient ruins of Nestor's Palace over on the hill. We could also see the small village of Pilos climbing up the hill on the southern end of the bay. After a week of anchoring we went to Pilos for fuel, water, and food. Our next passage was to be across the Ionian to Italy.

That passage was very slow for the wind was almost nonexistent. But it was nice. Right in the middle of the Ionian Sea I said to Janet,"Honey do you know what I crave? I crave a Big Mac!"

Janet said, "You've never had a Big Mac!"

"I know it, but I want one now!" She was right, I had never had one and I wasn't going to get one now.

We planned on entering Italy at Syracuse on Sicily, but that plan went out the window too. We picked up some good wind and hated to waste it, so on a beam reach we went up the Straits of Messina. We weren't going very fast, about 5 knots, but it was salubrious sailing. So we entered Italy at Reggio di Calabria, right on the big toe of the boot. We stayed there until we got our *constituto*, which is our permit to cruise Italian waters. It is given only after you have purchased Italian insurance. Ours cost $72.00 for one year but is probably much higher now.

While we were there in Reggio di Calabria, a very important government official was assassinated, allegedly by the Mafia. The next day we heard that the Italian Government had declared war on the Mafia. Roughly six months later the Mafia was winning. Casualties of the government were over 600. Casualties of

the Mafia were not announced but rumored to be very few.
Still wanting to see Sicily, we went around the northeastern tip of that island and into Milazzo. We tied up on the main dock which is very convenient to shops and bakeries. But as the town is full of oil refineries, the odor is pretty bad. So we stayed just three days and then left for the island of Vulcano.
This island has a different smell–sulfur. Not at all pleasant. Tourists would come down to the beach covered with mud from the pits at the base of the volcano, then they'd go into the bay and wash the mud off. We wondered if it made them better persons.
The smell eventually drove us out and it was on to Stromboli. This is called the "World's Oldest Lighthouse" because for 2500 years, it has been guiding sailors to the Straits of Messina. Unfortunately the night we were there the moon was full and we couldn't see the glow from the volcano. By the way, the anchorages there are dangerous, too deep, too close to shore, and too rough, so we were glad to leave the next day.
We went into many harbors along the Italian coast, but one of our favorites is Sapri, 80 miles from Stromboli. We entered it at dawn about 30 minutes ahead of a heavy rain storm. We went behind the new breakwater and dropped anchor. Except for us and the small fishing smacks there were no other boats in the harbor. Then the skies opened and it poured and thundered and the winds blew.
The next day, during a clear spell, a small motor boat circled us and then came back. Speaking in perfect English a lovely young lady asked, "Did you really sail that small boat from San Diego?" When we said that we had their boat came along side. The young lady had been an exchange student in Washington D.C. for two years and the young man was her fiance. We visited for a short time and then they asked us to dinner that night. They picked us up in the motor boat and we went to their favorite pizza restaurant and had Italian ice cream for dessert. Just another one of those nice experiences that seem to come our way.
On the following morning, during another clear spell, a small open boat came out from the hotel on the shore. In it were

three people who brought us hot espresso in a silver carafe and said "Welcome to Italy." We found the southern Italians to be very cordial and we liked them a lot.

The weather really fell apart as we sailed north up the coast of Italy. We went by the island of Capri, but couldn't see it, for the clouds were down almost to the water. Those clouds wiped out Vesuvius too as we sailed across the Bay of Naples. But we were able to see the buoyed channel that took us into the small bay at the northwestern end of the bay. Waiting out the weather took five days and it seemed interminable. Finally, there was a little blue sky showing so we took to the sea again.

We wanted to stop in Gaeta for the winter and that was our next destination. Some friends in Cyprus had wintered there for a rather small fee. It was also the home of the US Navy's 6th Fleet and there was a commissary and a post exchange (PX) there which made it doubly attractive. But that hope went for naught.

The marina owner wanted the equivalent of $500US each month just for putting our bow next to his dock. There were no amenities like electricity and showers and the commissary was miles away. So we paid for one night, shopped during the day, and then left.

We had miserable weather all the way north. Off Anzio it really worsened to gale force and we appeared to be the only boat out on the water. From this storm we spotted huge trees that had been uprooted, washed down by heavy force of water in the rivers and eventually into the Mediterranean. So we were delighted to finally spot the striped lighthouse that marked the entrance to Fumare Grande, the western end of the Tiber River. We went into the channel and motored carefully past all the fishing nets hanging from the shore on either side.

There were many boats in the river all moored to rather rickety docks. We saw no location that looked appealing, so we ventured through the channel again and north to the breakwaters shaping the entrance to the Fiumicino Canal. The canal is very short, only about 2 miles, with two bridges across it that close it off. With their permission, we tied next to a fishing boat as we waited for the bridges to open. They have a definite schedule, which seems to change now and then, so you must wait.

We went past the pedestrian bridge and through the one for cars. Off to our port side, just beyond the bridge, was a high wall to which several sailboats were tied and we heard the name of our boat being called out. Two of those boats were from Cyprus and we saw familiar faces. They waved to us to come alongside them and that we did.

We weren't certain that we could stay there for another sailboat had made a reservation and was expected in momentarily. After three days the other boat failed to show up, so we were given permission to stay. That was quite a relief for the charges were reasonable and the stores were close and the bus and train stops were right outside the main gate.

When we had come in to tie up, our engine made a dreadful noise. An Australian friend standing on the dock said "That has a very expensive sound!" And he was right. The engine's distributors near Rome came down and picked it up and the verdict wasn't good. We'd have to have a complete rebuilt one to replace the old motor. The trouble appeared to be the motor oil we bought in Bali. We knew the fuel was dirty, but we didn't think of the oil. It seems that they had refilled the proper jugs with linseed oil and that's what ruined our diesel. Swell! So, $5,700 later we got back a rebuilt engine. The only trouble was that they left out gaskets, "O" rings, and little things like that. We didn't find out about that until after a couple of months of the engine leaking fuel. But that's another story.

While the Fiumicino Canal wasn't much of a canal it served its purpose. We stayed there safely through the winter and enjoyed being within close range of Rome. It is a truly beautiful city, but the thievery had reached epidemic proportions. All the boaters around us had their pockets picked, but we didn't. Janet sewed up some linen envelopes with zippers that we wore around our necks. They held traveler's checks, our passports and cash. We believe that they saved us from the pickpockets.

However, Italy was the most expensive country we visited. We became very tired of the game played by the cashiers in stores and shops when we were shopping. Inevitably we would be short-changed, and when we argued about it a few more lira would be given, but the amount would still be short. The only place we felt that we wouldn't be cheated was at the Vatican and the local open market in Fiumicino. Once we even had to pay Customs duty to get our mail. It wasn't much, but it was the principle of the thing.

While there was much about Italy that appalled us, we did enjoy our stay at the marina. Except for one Sunday when the weather was absolutely horrid, we had a barbecue each weekend. All of the crews at Fiumicino came and many from Fumare Grande.

Remember back to 1985 when we had arrived outside of Sydney harbor on our 49th day? The New Zealand warship *Canterbury* was the first ship to come to our rescue. Well, coincidentally a young man had been a crewman on that warship. Now in 1990 here he was, a crewman on a very large yacht from New Zealand. As a souvenir he gave us his hat band from the HMS *Canterbury,* which I have to this day.

All of the time spent here was very companionable and the food at the BBQ's was delicious. But spring finally came and boats began to leave. Westerly winds blowing heavily kept everyone from sailing to Sardinia and Corsica. Those were to be our destinations, but we gave in to the prevailing winds and went north on a great beam reach. We went to Island of Giglio and anchored for two days, then it was on to Elba. That's a lovely island and we don't know why Napoleon felt he had to leave. We stayed four days as a wicked wind blew up and kept us in the harbor. We were tied to the main dock which was free, with shopping facilities near by.

Capraia was to be our next island after a pleasant day's sail. We anchored outside the marina in the open roadway just beneath a 1,000 year old castle. We were in sheltered waters and the holding was great so our stay there was a joy. But the time had come for us to begin our cruise of mainland Europe.

CHAPTER NINE

It was a night sail across the Gulf of Genoa. There was no moon and it was very dark. About noon the next day we saw many, many big sailboats tacking around off shore and we knew we were nearing Monaco. That lovely little principality was soon visible and we motored inside the harbor. We felt like a dinghy for we were surrounded by sailboats that all seemed to be at least 125 feet long. They were manned by uniformed crews who were scrubbing decks and polishing brass. One of the deepest and most expensive harbors in the Mediterranean–we shook our heads negatively as the harbormaster tried to wave us in to pick up a mooring. We sailed on about two miles away to Cap Ferret, anchored (for free) and looked back at the glory of Monaco.

There is no Port of Entry into France, but we felt we should let them know we were there. So we motored into the crowded harbor at Nice and picked up a slip at the yacht club. I took all of ship's papers and passports down to the harbormaster's office, but they really didn't want to see us. They did want one night's fee equivalent to about $28.00US for the slip, however. Thus began our very slow cruise along that spectacular coast of the Riviera. We had been told that we could go the entire length of southern France in three days. Sorry, it took us 6 weeks. We loved the gunkholes.

There were so many inviting coves and islands dotting the whole coast and we couldn't resist them. So in we'd sail, drop the anchor, and stay for three or four days. Delightful! We discovered one thing about the French boaters–they don't spend the night out aboard their boats. Once or twice we'd enter a very crowded bay or harbor and then watch in amazement that by the middle of the afternoon everyone was packing up to go home. That did make for peace and quiet.

Except for our stop in Nice, we entered no other cities along the coast of France. We knew that we would have to lower our mast at Port St. Louis du Rhone so began the passage to reach there. The Cote d' Azur is not nearly so pretty and inviting as the Riviera and, after so many pleasant stops there, we felt that nothing could top that, but we had reckoned without the inland waterways of Europe. Overwhelming!

We left the Mediterranean forever when we entered the canal leading to Port St. Louis. We tied up to the quay and I prepared to do what I could about our oil-leaking engine. The harbor was full of cruising boats, many with engine problems they were trying to straighten out. One boat had been there for two years and still wasn't repaired. Thanks to a young British sailor, who had an engine just like ours, and with spare parts, we were able to repair our engine enough and move on.

The laws have all changed now and we aren't certain what rules are in effect, so we can't give you any idea of what to expect. We do know that if you and your boat overstay your time you are charged an exorbitant import tax on your boat. But at the time we were there didn't seem to be any limit to our length of stay—although in Paris we were told that we could stay one year from the time our passports were stamped. As ours were never stamped, that seems to imply an indefinite time limit.

We hadn't planned to go through the canals and rivers of Europe when we left San Diego, but in Tel Aviv, Israel, we met a young Danish couple who encouraged us to do this. We felt we had too much draft, a little more than six feet, but they had more than that and had made the passage from Copenhagen to the Mediterranean five times. So we went looking for books and charts about the inland waterways. There weren't any to be had so we had to wait until we got to Port St. Louis.

From the harbor we went to Bayle's boatyard where we had our mast lowered. The bridges in Europe are quite low and even with the mast on top of the cabin roof we would sometimes have to hold our breaths for fear we wouldn't clear under the bridge. Remember that the canals were built for commercial boats (*peniches*) so they have the right of way over yachts.

Yachts have to pull to the side to get out of their way and inevitably get stuck in the mud. We always seemed to meet a *peniche* when the river and the canal was the most narrow.

Using the *Cartes du Fluvial* (Road maps of the river or canal) that we were able to buy in Port St. Louis, we tackled the Rhone and Saone Rivers with confidence. Yes, the huge locks were at first intimidating, but we soon became used to them and went through with ease. We made many stops going north with our favorites being Avignon and Lyon. While in Avignon the whole city was in celebration for the "Art Festival." Young talented people were all around, singing and playing instruments in bars, coffee shops, or any place where a few or more people were congregated. Looking over an artist's shoulder to see what he/she were painting didn't seem to make them nervous. They were there mainly to be and get recognized. The real talented ones always drew a crowd.

Janet told me that if Paris was anything like Lyon I might never get her out of France. We tied to the quay across from the big St. Jean Cathedral. There was a tall wall above the quay and on top of the quay was an open market that was open seven days a week. The variety of food there was quite incredible and the wonderful vendors would give us samples of their cheeses and salamis. And the fruit, vegetables and meat was excellent. But after 2 1/2 weeks it was time to enter the canals.

The Canal du Centre was fine–good and deep, but when we went into the Canal Lateral du Loire we bumpety-bumped along. And as we neared Decize we thought we'd never get through. There were sand and mud bars every few feet and we spent most of the day revving up the engine to get through. We went about two miles beyond Decize and tied to the bank for the night. And why were the canals so low? There had been a three year drought in the Loire Valley and the water was down 12 to 14 inches, so we bumped a lot. At the entrance to the lock leading to Nevers we tied to the dock. There we inflated our dinghy and off-loaded four anchors, a life raft, chain, lines and lots of odds and ends. This raised our waterline about two inches. It helped tremendously but not completely. We still became fast aground, sometimes taking hours to get through the sandbars.

One time we were thoroughly stuck. No matter how I turned the wheel and revved the engine we couldn't go forward, sideways, or backwards. A young man came jogging down the path alongside the canal. He said something in French turned around and jogged around the bend and disappeared. A few minutes he was backing a very small compact car down the path, stopped by us, and motioned for me to toss him a line. I tossed the bow line to him and I told Janet, "I sure hope he doesn't start off with a jerk and tear his rear end out." Soon he had the line tied, got in his car and gave me the signal to rev my engine. The line became taut, the boat quivered a bit and finally began to move and was finally free. I signaled him to stop and unhook my bow line. Janet and I both yelled "*Merci.*"

The young man was waving his arms and yelling, "*Bon voyage, bon voyage.*"

Once we crossed the Loire River, the water became deeper and we had no further problems. The small towns that we went through were delightful and many times we tied to stakes on the main street. People would speak to us as they walked by and we'd answer in our fractured French. But the lock keepers seemed to understand us. I would say, "Janet, you speak to the lock keeper." She would and the lock keeper would nod and do as she asked. It was a great arrangement.

Once we reached the Seine we knew we were close to what was to be our winter home, Paris. There are many good anchorages on the Seine and we used them each evening. The locks on the Seine weren't very tall, but they were quite long. And, horrors–one had sloping sides. Janet kept the engine running and tried to keep the boat in the middle of the lock while I, armed with a boat hook, fended off from the sides of the lock. It wasn't one of our favorite experiences and we were thankful when we saw the gates finally open. We just had to admit to ourselves that many canals and locks were not made for sailboats.

We knew we were in Paris when up ahead we could see Notre Dame Cathedral on an island in the river. Paris! At last. Janet was thrilled, for that had long been her dream. Now it had come true. Janet had always said that if I never took her to Paris, after she died she would come back and haunt me. Now I didn't have to worry about that anymore.

We went through the lock that took us into the Port du Plaisance de la Bastille, where we would spend the winter. It was almost full with boats from all over the world and many moored there permanently. This latter included several Americans. In fact, there were 19 of us who celebrated Thanksgiving day with a big turkey dinner aboard a *peniche* owned by a retired California school teacher. Janet baked the pumpkin pies for the dinner and all the others contributed dishes. It was a very nice day. We American Pilgrims had come to Paris.

Paris was very expensive as far as food and supplies are concerned, but transportation and other niceties were quite reasonable. We went all over on the Paris subway (the Metro) for very little cost. But we soon learned not to try and buy American products for the prices were out of sight. For example: Stove Top Dressing was about $8.00US. Also another good rule was never to order anything in a French restaurant without learning the price first. Otherwise you could be in for a shock.

We had to go to the American Embassy to sign some papers for Social Security as Janet had reach the magic "65." It was noon time when we left the Embassy and we were getting hungry. I had to stop at the big BHV store (similar to WalMart). We took the subway for convenience. Getting off at the required stop for the big store we came up out of the subway and guess what we saw? In case you haven't guessed–it was the Golden Arches of McDonalds. We are ashamed to say, but our very first meal in the Cuisine Capital of the World was a Big Mac. My first Big Mac and I enjoyed it. But in France you can have beer or wine, so I topped it off with a beer.

Another time we were shopping and noon time was close, so we decided to have a croissant and a cup of cappuccino. We went in and ordered. A Canadian couple came in and, as there was no more table room, we invited them to sit with us. They ordered the special which was advertised on a billboard out front on the sidewalk. Shrimp or something fishy–can't remember. All enjoyed the food until we got the bill. The specialty was the equivalent of $100.00US a plate. Our croissant and cappuccino came at $25.00US each. After that you can be sure we always inquired about the prices, before sitting down.

Everywhere you looked in Paris you saw only beauty. But beauty is always in the eye of the beholder, so the beauty we saw may not have been the beauty to you that we experienced. The architecture is world renowned and worth every word of praise. And the Louvre is beyond description. And speaking of the Louvre, Janet was having trouble walking, so we got a wheel chair so could then sit and ponder great art. We wanted to see the Mona Lisa but it was in a small anteroom. There was a line of people THAT long. The attendant saw us at the back of the line and motioned us forward past all the people patiently standing to come forward. It really didn't seem fair that we barge ahead of all those people. We found then and there what a great advantage a disabled person has over able bodied people.

The only building we thought was ugly is the new Pompidou Center on the Right Bank. It looks like a whole bunch of sewer pipes welded together. It took the place of the famous Les Halles open market that had long served the excellent onion soup. The people who live around there are grateful that the market is gone for they said that it attracted hundreds of rats. We saw none at this date.

What more can we say about Paris except that it's Paris? Janet reveled in it as she loved the whole city. It had long been her dream. And the people. We were told, "You won't like the French. They are rude, sometimes crude, and not a bit friendly." We found that to be so much hogwash. We met many French people who have become endeared friends and we have corresponded with them ever since.

We left Paris in the company of two other sailboats, one American, and one Canadian. We went into the Marne together and made many of the same stops. But occasionally we would miss each other and then, hey, there they are. Our draft was greater than that of the other two boats so they could get into harbors and marinas that we couldn't. This is one thing that angered us about the canals: if you're required to have no more than a 1.8 meter draft then all the anchorages and marinas should be at least 1.8. No way! At times the depths would be posted on a sign and it was nearly always 1.1 meter or less. Unfortunately the Cartes don't give the depths and if none was posted we had to go in with a lead line. Yes, we have a depth gauge, but it's in the middle of the boat which is no good when you're going in bow first. While you cannot anchor in any of the canals, you can anchor in rivers and we did that as often as possible. But occasionally we'd have to tie up somewhere, with our stern sticking out, to get fuel and water.

Just before we entered the Marne au Rhin Canal, a young lock-keeper handed to us a list of the charges about to be imposed by the Canal Authority. He seemed embarrassed. The charges aren't cheap and they'll be for one day, week, month, season, or year. You'll be charged by the length, depth, and beam of your boat and that can add up to a lot of dollars. We feel that it will cut down enormously on the number of boats going through France.

And there's bound to be a lot of anger when people must pay for a day that they spent waiting for a malfunctioning lock to open. We think that all the towns along the canals will suffer as the number of boats drops. Yachties do spend money, but now they won't be spending much time along the way

The other two boats with us paid but we didn't. When we got to Toul (a free harbor at that time), an officer with the Canal Authority told us not to pay the charges. He said, "No, they're confused. No one knows how much to charge or who to pay it to." So we went on with a clear conscience.

The scenery along the Marne au Rhin river and canal was very pleasant. Lovely villages in charming settings. Then you come to the Mauvage Tunnel which is another story all together. Going right through a mountain, it's only three miles long, but it takes 1 3/4 hours to go through it. And that's 1 3/4 hours of pure hell.

All of the boats are tied in a line with 100 foot long lines between them. The *peniches* go first and all yachts last. As many of the lights inside the tunnel aren't working it's very dark. All we could see was the stern light of the huge *peniche* ahead of us as we moved slowly forward. That was rather scary, but even moreso was the sound of the *peniches* hitting the sides of the 200 year old tunnel. The sides were all shored up as they were in the process of collapsing. And the top wasn't in great condition either. The water poured down on top of us. We wondered if this was to be the day that the Mauvage Tunnel collapsed. As there is no ventilation, you can't use your engine, so you have to bear the slow pace. This is certainly not the place for a claustrophobic person. Never have we felt such relief as we did when we saw the sunlight at the end of the tunnel. Whew!

From the Marne au Rhin River and Canal we entered the Moselle River. This must be the most beautiful inland waterway in the world. From rolling hills covered with vineyards to ancient castles, forts, and chateaus around every bend, the views were spectacular. Each stop was an even greater joy. Eastern France is very special.

In Toul, we had some mechanical parts to repair and enjoyed the few days spent in several peoples' company. A single man of about thirty kept bringing us bottles of wine and cheese. He apologized for his terrible English. I said, "Don't apologize for your English, your accent is beautiful. If you were in the America, you could go to a night club and have a girl on each knee and a swarm of beauties all around you." He said, "Goodbye, I'm leaving tomorrow morning very early for America."

Toul, France was a beautiful, people-orientated little town. They had a Mayor who hired a "town landscape gardener." The gardeners' salary were the highest in town except for the mayor. I'm sure he earned his keep as each grave in the cemetery was decorated with fresh flowers every day, and all the monuments, etc., (and there were many from both World Wars) were always kept clean, bannered and with flowers displayed when a public parade or other ceremonies were taking place. The short time we were there it seemed there was something public going on almost everyday.

We left France on the Moselle River that runs between Germany and Luxembourg. In France it is the Moselle, in Germany and Luxembourg it becomes the Mosel. The customs office on the German border was closed; it was a Sunday. We stopped and then motored on. More vineyards and picturesque villages with the ubiquitous castles and forts. Many vineyards we saw were on such steep slopes we wondered how they ever picked the grapes without tumbling downhill. We never got tired of seeing them. As we usually tied to the quay in the center of each village a lot of people would stop and talk to us. We enjoyed that very much.

When we first entered Germany we were not certain how the Germans would react to our American flag. After all, we bombed the daylights out of them in World War II. But we needn't have worried. They were warm, genuinely hospitable,and affectionate. Most of them told us that they were so glad that the Americans got there before the Russians did. Along the way we met two Germans who had been POWs and sent to the United States. Both said that if they had known how good the food was in the States, they would've surrendered much sooner. The Germans were very nice to us.

At each of our stops along the German rivers, we expected to stay just over night, but that wasn't to be. Hospitality would overwhelm us and we'd end up staying for four or five days. One day the wind seemed to be right on our nose, cold and very uncomfortable. We had been going since early morning and now at noon I said to Janet, "If we can find a wide spot in the river and deep enough let's stop for the rest of the day." Just around the bend we found it. It was 18 feet deep. It was a grand spot as it was away from all the river traffic, so we dropped the hook. We made certain that we would not drag the anchor.

No sooner had we poured ourselves a glass of wine and sat down in the cockpit when there was a knock on the hull. We looked over the side and there sat two German men. They greeted us in English and said, "We came out to welcome you to our little club for a beer and a barbecued steak dinner, will you please come?" It took us about two seconds before we could enter their dinghy and the motored us to the Oberfell Sailing Club.

At the little Oberfell Sailing Club, we were invited to take part in their national regatta. Janet christened two new boats and we took part in potluck suppers and parties. We were also driven all over that part of Germany. And when we went to Koblenz on the Rhine, the people from Oberfell came down each day to make certain that we were being treated all right. One young couple make us a very serious invitation to come spend Christmas with them. That invitation was a very hard one to turn down, because these people were so cordial, warm and I know we would have had the time of our lives.

In Koblenz we were able to buy the charts for the German canals. They were very clearly written in German but understandable. We had to be in Dusseldorf by June 15 to meet some friends who were joining us from Long Beach, California. They were going on the canals with us to Berlin, so we began our passage down the Rhine. The current in the Rhine is about six knots and our motor was pushing us at six knots, so we really flew down the Rhine. We made just two stops–one at Bad Honeff where we stayed for four days, and another in the rather dingy harbor of Koln (Cologne).

Big boat traffic on the Rhine is fast and plentiful, but we had no problems until just before entering the harbor at Dusseldorf. We were getting ready to go under the designated arch of a bridge with heavy traffic coming the other direction. To our right were red buoys marking the edge of the channel and we were as close to them as we could go without going aground. Behind us a huge *peniche* came barreling along, honking his horn and waving at us to move aside. We couldn't, there was no room and the forward traffic was bearing down. So we held our course until we could turn to starboard and into the Dusseldorf harbor. The *peniche* captain waved his fist at us angrily, and we were still trying to figure out what he wanted us to do. Janet unceremoniously shook her fist back at him.

We stayed in Dusseldorf for ten days. A very dear friend in San Diego and some cousins that had lived all their lives here.

When we called them, Dusseldorf was ours. We were given the red carpet treatment. The a newspaper reporter wanted to interview us for his paper. We asked him why so many people were staring down at us from the dock. He said that there roughly 200,000 people in Dusseldorf and that we were the first American sail boat ever to enter. I think the whole 200,000 came down to stare at us the minute his article was on the street.

With our friends on board who joined us to travel, we went to Berlin via the Mittelland Canal. The greater part of the Mittelland Canal was in the old sector of East Germany and had hardly changed much since the Berlin wall was torn down. Much of the canal was quite rural. We saw several deer along the banks and a couple swimming. We could see where brush and growth was coming back and in some areas there were machine gun emplacements still in place, and some barbed wire laying around.

While in Berlin we stayed at the US Army Marina on the Wannsee. We understand that it was being closed at the end of 1994, but we were grateful it was open when we were there. The harbor officials told us that we were one of two boats visiting, the very first American cruising boats ever to visit their harbor. The other cruising American power boat arrived a few days after we entered port. It was owned by a member of San Diego Yacht Club. Small world. All the other boats were owned by American servicemen who had bought their boats in Berlin or had them shipped in.

We think that Berlin is the most beautiful city we have visited. An American naval officer who drove us around confessed that, to him, the most beautiful city in Europe was Prague. But since we didn't get to Prague, we'll have to take his word for it. However, we'll stick with Berlin, at least what was formerly West Berlin. So many fountains, parks, and trees that it was hard to take it all in. And, once again, the Germans we met were delightful.

We had planned to go east to the Oder River in Poland and down to the Baltic Sea. But we stayed so long in Berlin that we had to make different plans. The Oder was down to a trickle and it was too late to go into the Baltic as the autumn weather was socking in. So we went west again on the Elbe-Havel Canal until we reached the Niegripp Schleuse (lock).There we ran into trouble. The Elbe was out of water and we were aground in the middle of the canal leading to the lock. The Wasser Polizei (water police) towed us around in the small lake, plowing a small furrow on the bottom sand with our keel and we tied to an old *peniche* for the two months and five days we were there.The Mittelland Canal had three meters of water, but we couldn't get to it; just 10 kilometers away. So close, yet so far.

The engineer at the lock owned the *peniche* we were tied to, and he came running down to plug us into his electricity and to bring several jugs of water. For all the time we were there he and his wife and their family and friends treated us as if we were their family. They were marvelous to us and once more we were overwhelmed with kindness.

We could not speak or understand German, and 99% of the people here did not speak or understand English. Remember they were under Russian domination for 45 years. The Russians forbade learning English but made it mandatory that they learn Russian. However, communication was relatively easy as I had the Klinna (little) book and Manny had the Grossa (big) book. The books took care of the basics, but sign language took over and we communicated quite well. Oh! there were no serious discussion about politics, religion etc. Except on one occasion, I asked Manny, "What did you think of the Russians while they occupied your country?"

Manny answered in one word, "Gestunken!" I didn't have to look that word up to know what it meant. All the surrounding little and big cities, showed the devastation that World War II had caused. Under Russian domination there was little or no reconstruction done as was in west Germany by the allied forces. There was no love lost between the Germans and the Russians. The news media made a splash about us and people from all around the area, began dropping in to see us, inviting us to their homes and their yacht club and of course we had to exchange burgies. Although we were anxious to get going it was hard to turn down the hospitality these Germans were giving us. What fond memories we have of this area.

The water in the Elbe continued to drop, much to our despair. According to our German friends, the water would continue to drop until it rained and filled the rivers in the Czech Republic (Czechoslovakia) then they'd run over into the east German rivers. But the skies stayed blue and there wasn't a single drop of rain. We were beginning to wonder how they celebrated Christmas in Germany when, at the beginning of November, the rains came and the Elbe began to fill.

On November 5 a Canal Authority boat, the *Hecht,* tied us alongside of them and took us down to the giant Hebewerk lock near Magdeburg. To me, the Hebewerk lock was a modern day miracle of German engineering. The lock, like a gigantic bathtub, was about the size of an American football field with a depth of probably 12 feet or more and was raised and lowered by four huge steel screws. The screws were probably one and a half to two feet in diameter and over 90 feet long. Each screw had to be synchronized perfectly with the others to lift many thousands of tons of weight. The lock worked like an elevator, hoisting or lowering as many as six *peniches* and other small boats in just a matter of a few minutes.

Many of our friends came down to see us off. Fortunately Janet had prepared a large pot of pinto beans. She made a bunch of "hushpuppies" to go with the beans. Also we had an assortment of good German wines which we served. Those Germans licked their soup bowls clean and ask for more, never having eaten like that in their life. Fortunately the company was begging off on their third batch of hushpuppies and the last of the beans. We went up in the lock, tied to the dock for the night and the next morning entered the Mittelland Canal once more.

The scenery had changed quite a bit since we were last in those waters. The tree leaves had changed color and were falling and the gun emplacements along the canal had been removed, but there was still some barbed wire visible. There seemed to be an awful lot of barge traffic, some of it moving very slowly. One day we got stuck behind one and just poked along, to our annoyance. The weather was very cold and we wanted to get to our winter home in the Netherlands and turn on the heater.

By the time we reached Munster the weather just fell apart. It was so bad that there were white caps on the canal. Not only did we stop for two days, but, also, all the commercial traffic stopped. The wind finally died, but the rains continued and as we reached the first lock on the Wesel Canal there was a cloud burst. Although there had been nothing behind us we were very leery as we stopped dead in the middle of the channel because we couldn't see. Then the rain stopped, and we entered the Wesel Canal and began our passage to the Rhine once more.

CHAPTER TEN

With the six knot current on the Rhine and our diesel pushing us at six knots we really zipped along the 45 kilometers to the Netherlands border. Just across we saw a sign that read "Netherlands Customs," so we turned to starboard and entered the small harbor. The Dutch Customs officer was very nice and made entering easy. Present in his office was a German Customs officer who officially signed us out of Germany although we hadn't officially entered Germany.

We had chosen the Ijssel Canal for our transit north to the Ijsselmeer in the Netherlands. There are no locks on the Ijssel Canal and, frankly, we were tired of locks. The Dutch Customs officer had told us that there were plenty of coves along the canal where we could anchor, but there weren't. We did find entrances to yacht harbors but they were too shallow for us. Twice we got stuck in the mud and had to motor away from that place. Twice was enough so we didn't try that again.

What the Customs officer was possibly referring to were the low dams built out from the shore toward the middle of the canal. While on the Rhine we had seen them and had been told they were to slow down the current and keep the soil on the edge of the river from being washed away. Perhaps they served the same purpose in the canal.

When night fell we pulled into one of the small coves and dropped the anchor. I had to put out three anchors, for the holding, in soft mud was terrible. The wash from the passing barges and *peniches* didn't help and neither did the already filled quays in the many villages we passed. Commercial vessels had reached there first so on we went, regretfully for many of the villages looked so inviting. But winter was coming and we wanted to reach our goal as soon as possible. That goal was the marina at

Enkhuizen where we had reservations and where our Brit cruising friends were waiting for us. We had called them from the Dutch Customs office to let them know that we were on our way. Entering the Ijsselmeer (formerly the Zuider Zee) was a bit of a shock. After having nice weather on the canal, we suddenly faced a Force 7-8 gale. The wind was pushing us backwards so we had to run the diesel at full bore in order to make any forward progress. And the waters were so rough that we never did see the small green buoys that marked the safe channel. Consequently we touched bottom three times, but pulled right off. Finally, far ahead, Janet saw a red buoy sticking up. We circled it and it was the right one marking the beginning of the channel to Enkhuizen and there were the leading lights.Immediately upon entering the channel we turned to starboard through the breakwater marking the entrance to the marina. There, ahead on the dock, were our Brit friends waiting for us with an invitation to dinner. What more could we ask?

Enkhuizen was really a wonderful place to spend the winter. The town was charming and quaint, criss-crossed with canals, and the people were so friendly. It wasn't quite as cold as we expected, being just 15 miles from the North Sea, but the marina waters did freeze over once for a couple of days. It was a shock one morning to wake up and see people ice skating around the boats. There were three boats with winter live-aboards and those Captains had to use boat hooks each morning to chop the ice away from the through-hull fittings.

Our cat Tigger loved the cold weather. He had developed a thick coat of beautiful black fur so he was warm. It never did really snow, but one day there were some flurries and Tigger reveled in it–frolicking in the snow and trying to catch snowflakes as they fell and blew around. It was a delight to watch him.

We spent another lovely Christmas with our Brit friends and took many auto trips with them. They had gone to England and brought their car back with them, which was convenient. We did dearly love the shopping in Holland. The supermarkets were that–super, and there were so many small shops where you could find myriad items to buy. Most of which you didn't need, but were interesting to look at. Oh, but they had the best sausages we had ever tasted. Also I found the German wine, Swartzen Katz, that I liked so well. The little German town where I first heard of the wine had run out, so I had to do with other less tasty brands.

Janet had problems with her legs, which was what kept us in Germany so long, and it got progressively worse. A Dutch friend took her to a doctor in Enkhuizen and he couldn't find a pulse in her right leg. He called the AMC (Amsterdam Medical Center) and made arrangements for her to go in immediately. She entered the hospital and the verdict was that the femoral artery in her right leg was blocked. They tried to open it with a balloon, but that didn't work, so they scheduled her for surgery.

After the surgery she came down with a bad bacterial infection an insidious disease and was very seriously ill. They called me through some very good friends and told them to bring me in to the hospital as quickly as possible. After a drive of sixty miles, I arrived at the hospital. There the doctor said that unless a miracle occurred Janet wouldn't live through the night. I asked the doctor if any miracles had ever happened in the hospital before. The doctor wasn't certain but he believe there had been a couple before this time. Then I said, "Well doctor let's pray there will be one more happening tonight." When I walked into her room, all I could see were the hoses, wires and machines that were keeping her alive. She had two cardiac arrests, kidney and liver failure, and her blood pressure was 50/30.

The hospital gave me a room right down the hall from Janet and a chit so that I could eat in the cafeteria. At the end of six days Janet started to come out of it and two days later she was taken out of intensive care. The doctor that had greeted me the first night was now all smiles. I told him that it looked like another miracle had happened. He said, "Yes, we were all keeping our fingers crossed there for a few days." But the infection was still with her; she spent two months in the hospital and they watched her like a hawk. Her hospital care couldn't have been any better. We had high praise for the whole staff even down to the housekeepers. Everyone was very cordial. Maybe it is because they were Dutch. When they released her the doctor told her to get home (San Diego) as soon as possible. She was certain he meant a 747, and he was quite upset to hear that she was sailing home. His answer, "Well, if you need another bypass in the middle of the ocean we can't help you."

While Janet was in the hospital, I had the boat hauled out of the water for bottom painting and a few repairs. Our Brit friends helped. When that was finished and the boat was back at the marina, I had the mast re-stepped and had a GPS (Geographical Positioning Satellite) installed. This electronic device took the place of the time-worn SATNAV. It updated our position every ten seconds and is accurate at very close range. Much better than the old SATNAV, the GPS was new and issued to soldiers in the Gulf War. Since Desert Storm the price has dropped enough to be affordable which is a real boon to sailors.

We left Enkhuizen the middle of May and began our passage down the mast-up canals of the Netherlands. As we'd had the mast raised at Enkhuizen it was nice to be a sailboat again, even though we couldn't use the sails in the canals. But the trip south was a delight. We crossed the Ijsselmeer and went to Hoorn the first night. Then it was down to Amsterdam. We found the very small and crowded Sixhaven Marina and stayed three days. We had friends in Amsterdam that we visited, then we went west to the canal leading to Haarlem.

All of our stops in Holland were pleasant as there was nearly always a place to tie up for the night. The only delay was waiting for bridges and locks to open, but we didn't mind that too much as there was always some place to tie up. We finally reached Vlissingen (Flushing), the southernmost town in the Netherlands and we bypassed the marina. We had been warned that it was terribly crowded and expensive so we went into the main harbor.

There we tied to the quay until a crewman from the huge crane barge came and told us we'd have to move, as two other barges were coming in. He told us to tie to their stern and use their electricity and water at no cost. That was a splendid offer and that's what we did. Janet baked several batches of chocolate chip cookies for the crew of the barge and they were most grateful. Chocolate chip cookies are purely American, and no other country has them.

After seven days the weather finally improved to the point where we dared to venture out into the North Sea. It was a very short sail to Ostend, Belgium and the North Sea Yacht Club and it was so good to be under sail again. The next day we followed the chart and the buoyed channel to Dunkirk, France. Remembering the newsreel photos of WW II that showed boats going aground on the sand in the shallow waters around Dunkirk we knew that we didn't dare drift too close to the shore. Up ahead we could see the long high docks on either side of the channel leading into the inner Dunkirk harbor and we went in between them.

For some reason we had expected the city of Dunkirk to be larger than it was. But the harbor was pleasant and we had a good night's sleep. Early the next morning we left for Boulogne, France, and we had our first experience with the tides in the English Channel. It wasn't welcome.

We had long debated whether to risk the French coast in the Channel or go over to the English side. Our Dutch friends urged us to try the English side for the tides are less swift than on the southern coast. Also there are fewer rocks to dodge. So we crossed the Channel to the north side and came out a little east of Brighton, England. The tides off of England may be less swift, but they still pushed us back. I said that I knew we had passed that one lighthouse at least three times and we probably had.

Just as we were going past the south coast of the Isle of Wight a control wire on our wind vane broke. "That does it!" I said. I turned on the diesel and we went north up the east Coast of the Isle. I hate to steer so we took turns. We entered the channel to Portsmouth Harbor and picked up a mooring buoy. It was a lovely night.

The next day we were invited to go to the guest moorings at the Hardway Sailing Club and we accepted. It was a very nice and friendly club and we stayed four days. At the invitation of the club we spent many happy hours drinking Irish stout.

Then it was back to the Solent and west along the north coast of the Isle of Wight. We went into Newton Center anchorage with quite a bit of difficulty. All the way down the Solent the red buoys had been on our port side and the green ones to starboard and right in the middle of the Newton Channel was a red buoy. We were under sail and Janet was at the wheel at that time. She said that she'd leave the red buoy to port as she normally did and I agreed.

WRONG! A sand hillock was covered by water and we hit it at a good speed. We were definitely stuck. As our engine had died right outside of Portsmouth we couldn't power off, so there we sat, very embarrassed. That bay dries out at low tide and we really began to tilt. The Harbormaster saw our plight and came out in a dinghy with an outboard. He said he'd keep an eye on our mast and when it straightened he'd come out and tow us in to the anchorage. We had heeled way over on our side before the tide began to come back in. The result was water poured in at the gunwale area and there wasn't a thing we could do but run the bilge pump which didn't keep up with the in flow, so a lot of things were wet and ruined. He laughed when we told of our embarrassment and he said that a lot of Brits did the same thing. And so they did: we saw a couple of other boats in the same situation a few days later.

The anchorage was a good place to stop, and, besides, we had a large supply of books and clothes to dry out. Our lap top computer and other electrical or electronic equipment was ruined.

One morning we heard a shout. "Frank and Janet McNeill, what are you doing here?" It was a young couple that we'd wintered with in Fiumicino, Italy. They were on their way home from a three week cruise around the Scilly Islands. They anchored next to us and we had three nice days talking over old times.

When we left Newton, we went down the Solent, past the Needles and into the English Channel. Ever since we'd entered the Channel the weather had been horrible and it hadn't improved. But the tides west of the Isle of Wight seemed less swift than those to the east and we weren't pushed back. We went out to Start Point and then crossed the Channel once again. Thanks to the good tidal charts and our new GPS, we entered the Chanel du Four right on the button and zipped through at seven knots with the tide. We'd had two rough days so we pulled into the harbor at Cammaret for the night. The next morning we caught the tide and motored down the Brest Estuary and into the Moulin Blanc Marina.

Our good friends from Tahiti were now in Brest and we spent two weeks visiting with them. They were just as nice in Brest as they were in Tahiti, and we enjoyed ourselves with them. Then it was time to say goodbye again. That's one of the few negatives about cruising–you must say goodbye to good friends.

We went west in the Brest Estuary until we were out into the Bay of Biscay. The Bay has a terrible reputation and it wasn't at all nice to us after that first day. Once again our engine died after leaving Brest, so we were sailing south. The motor really needed a tune up, as we had put several thousand miles on it going through the rivers and canals of France, Germany and the Netherlands. But time did not permit this most needed maintenance. And because a gale was blowing I didn't dare take the heavy covers off and work on the engine. Things move around in the boat especially in gale force weather.

I soon had to put up storm sails as the wind increased to Force 8. Except for one day when the wind didn't blow and the fog was down to the water, we had gale force winds all the way to Spain.

The morning we arrived at the harbor at La Corunna, our batteries were very low and we noticed that our running lights were so weak you could barely see them up close, so we turned them off. We were a menace to navigation as many fishing boats and other big ships were coming and going. So we kept a very sharp lookout and didn't give any ship a chance to have a collision with us. We were inside the outer harbor about a mile from the breakwater entrance to the inner harbor when the wind died completely. What do we do now? We just sat there waiting for a ship or small boat to come by to ask them for a tow into the Yacht Club. We bobbed around a bit but as there was no current or wind we were accentually in the same spot at 3:00 P.M. as we were at 9:00 A.M.

According to the chart the outer harbor was too deep for safe anchoring. I said, "As no boats have come within shouting or signaling distance to us in all this time, I think we should call the harbormaster and see if someone can come tow us to the club." It wasn't long until we could see a fifty-foot boat coming to our rescue. Very expertly they towed and tied us up to the club in about thirty minutes time. They wanted all the particulars on my insurance, documentation etc.

Two days later I received word that I must see the Harbor Police. When I arrived I was handed an order signed by a judge that I was to pay the equivalent of $2,950.00 for the towing service. I was given 15 days in which to pay or the fee might increase. I immediately went to the American Consulate (who happened to be a Spaniard being paid by the U.S. Government. I camped on his door step for ten days, calling the company of the towing service (contracted by the Harbor Police) headquartered in Cadiz, the American Embassy in Madrid, calling our insurance company in Florida, and anyone I thought could help. The insurance company would only pay up to $500.00. The towing company would not listen to any negotiation, the American Embassy couldn't help unless I was thrown in jail, and they weren't quite sure about that.

At the end of ten days, I had made arrangement to pay the money by a special Master Card advance. Before I got to the bank to withdraw the money, I was summoned to the police again. Again, I was handed another order signed by the same judge stating that even though the fifteen days were not up, he had increased the fees to $4,000.00US.

I was furious. I came back to the boat, explained what had happened, and said, "Janet I want you to pack a quick bag. I'm taking you to the airport for the first flight out. You are going home. I am going to up anchor about midnight tonight and flee this stink hole. If we stay here much longer, who knows how high they will raise the fee or might even impound our boat.

Janet said, "You will not put me on any plane and I'm not leaving without you. If you go to jail, we both will go to jail. When do you think it will be safe to leave?"

Fortunately, our motor and other equipments had received proper maintenance, we had topped off the fuel and provisioned the boat. About 11:30 PM that night, I, quietly as possible, raised the anchor without too much noise and we motored out of the harbor. Then we went back into the Bay of Biscay, which was now calm. Several fishing boats were following us and we just knew one had to be from the police, but none were. It was very spooky and we were nervous wrecks for a couple of days. We went west to Latitude 8 Degrees in the Atlantic. We followed it due south to the Madeira Archipelago. It must have been the migrating season for whales, for we saw so many of them. One pod came very close to us. Just curious we thought. After a week of sailing, we pulled into the harbor on the island of Porto Santo. That island belonged to Portugal.

Just 40 miles from the big island of Madeira it's a different world. The village has just 5,000 people, but everything you need is there. Shopping was easy and the people were so friendly; we spent a very pleasant few months in Porto Santo.

As Janet wasn't certain that she'd be of much help to me, after her surgery in the Netherlands we'd asked my brother, Jeff, to join us for the return sail to San Diego. He flew in to Lisbon, Madeira, and then Porto Santo. We were very glad to see him and we thought he was quite brave. He was 78 years old and had never sailed before, but he came to help anyway. We couldn't have made it without him for having three people to stand night watches made life much easier.

During World War II Jeff had been in the U. S. Army stationed in New Guinea and surrounding territory. His experience was only in large troop carrying ships both to and from the combat areas. His association with salt water had been a few years in San Francisco for a few of his younger years–but never to do any sailing. He had spent the majority of his life in and around the

Denver area. He said to me once, "Frank, all the rest of the family have lived and been well satisfied with living in the mountainous state of Colorado, where did you get the genes to travel on the ocean?"

On the thirtieth of October, the worst storm in over a hundred years hit the Madeira Archipelago, which consisted of the main islands of Madeira and Porto Santo and several smaller islands which were not inhabited. But for the main islands there were five people killed and multi-millions of dollars damage to businesses, homes, public properties, and several small craft sunk and/or badly damaged. Our boat having gone through one hurricane and many fierce gales, came through again, but not without sustaining about $7,000.00 damage. We hurriedly made temporary repairs so we could be on our way.

We left Porto Santo on December 17 for the 3,500 mile passage to Antigua on the eastern edge of the Caribbean. We didn't want to make any stops, so we plotted a course to the west of the Canary and Cape Verde Islands heading at an angle for 17 degrees latitude. A stop at the Canary Islands may have brought the police down on us as they are Spanish owned. Remember, we are now fugitives from Spanish "Injustice." When we reached the 17th latitude we followed it due west. All along the way in the Atlantic we had seen two cruise ships, one other sailboat, one submarine, and two freighters. Except for a storm five days out of Porto Santo we had good weather and good winds all the way.

However, one day we were in the midst of another gale. Janet and I were taking it in our usual stride. Jeff was strapped on with his safety harness in the cockpit as he had been told to do and hanging on. Janet asked him, "Jeff are you O.K? Are you afraid?"

His reply was, "Yes I'm O.K. You and Frank don't seem to be afraid, so I'm not afraid either. I'm uncomfortable with the motion of the boat but I guess that goes with the territory. But after we get to San Diego, nothing less than the QE2 for me."

On the 29th day we anchored in English Harbor, Antigua, West Indies. There had been some bad weather, but It had been a great and fast crossing.

We stayed in Antigua for two weeks, enjoying the company of long-time cruising friends that we had last seen in Istanbul. While that island is very pleasant it is very expensive. Jeff was anxious to take Janet and me to breakfast one morning at the hotel. I will never forget that breakfast; Janet and I got our very foreign breakfast of "kippers." Jeff won't forget it either as the bill came to about $65.00. But do indulge in the English Harbor rum and the Antigua pineapples. They have no core, you just peel, slice across and eat. A true taste delight.

We'll give the Caribbean to anyone that wants it. It proved to be a very uncomfortable little body of water. While crossing it we went under storm sails all the way from Antigua to the Panama Canal. It was no fun at all. On the wind charts there's an area marked in red off the coast of Columbia and a note that says there are 15 foot waves there. Sorry about that, but the waves were more like 20-25 foot. A rough sail. But then we didn't harbor hop, we went straight to Panama, 1200 miles away.

On the 10th day we saw the towers marking the entrance to the harbor at Colon and the beginning of the Panama Canal. It was a good feeling.

CHAPTER ELEVEN

Panama was a bit of a culture shock. When you check in with the authorities, you are given a map that shows where it's safe to walk, but only in the day time. At night you venture out at your own risk. Crime is rampant in Panama and everyone tries very hard NOT to be a victim.

We tried to find space at the Panama Canal Yacht Club, but they were all filled up. So it was back to the Flats and anchoring in 40 feet of water. There were many boats anchored there, but no crowding, with lots of room to swing and the holding was good. You must anchor within the area marked by the yellow buoys, but that's no problem.

It was very interesting to watch all the boats as they passed by on their way through the canal. The big, beautiful cruise boats always drew our attention. There were so many of them. The charges for transiting the canal were horrendous, but we guess they made it back in passenger ticket fees.

The ad measurer came out to measure our boat and assess our charges and then we were ready to begin our transit. It was six days after we arrived when our pilots—we had two of them—came on board as well as two Panamanian line handlers. The pilots had to pass stringent tests and assist another pilot many times before he was given the opportunity of taking a ship through the canal on his own. The senior pilot had graduated to the point of being commissioned to take large vessels through. He just sat and advised the younger pilot (his assistant) who had almost the amount of credits to be on his own. Their salaries were paid by the Canal Authority. The Canal Authority collects fees from all boats going through the canal.

There must be four line handlers aboard. Two for the bow and two for the stern. Also the skipper of the boat must furnish four lines that are a minimum of 100 feet each. The lines must be strong enough to hold you in place should there be any turbulence or stray currents. My brother Jeff and I made up for the other two line handlers. The native line handlers were the sons of a waitress at the yacht club and had made the trip many times before. The charges for them was $40.00 each and they spent the night aboard, sleeping in the cockpit. And we supplied their meals.

All the boats are lined up and you take your turn going through the canal. The Canal Authority lets you know in plenty of time before you go through. The first lock looked intimidating, but it wasn't. Our pilots directed us to tie up alongside a Canal Authority launch and that we did, doing exactly as told. The lock began to fill and we were going up.

There weren't many yachts in the lock with us, but there was a large freighter. The commercial boats go into the "up" locks first, and second in the "down" ones, but we had little turbulence when the freighter fired up its motors.

We had heard of and read about all kinds of horror stories from people who had transited the canal, but we had no difficulties. Our pilots were very professional and we had faith in them. Not misplaced, we might add. Just a short distance outside the second lock, we turned to port and went into an anchorage for the night. Normally boats travel further on the first day, but the usual anchorage was being dredged, hence our short trip. On the second day we went past many small islands in Lake Gatun and into some wider waterways. These latter were all clearly marked with buoys and, besides, we had a new pilot to keep us on the right track. The scenery along the way was quite beautiful with many green trees and lots of foliage. Almost jungle-like in spots. We passed several small settlements and many canal boats that were hard at work. It was so very different from the monotony and barrenness of the Suez Canal.

At one point we came to the assistance of a small power boat that was doing some fishing. His engine had died, and he was having difficulty rowing an awkward boat to a buoy. Our pilot radioed for a Canal Authority boat to come and tow him as apparently the engine wouldn't start.

We finally sighted the last two locks and knew that we would soon be back in the Pacific Ocean, so we entered the anchorage at the Balboa Yacht Club with excitement. We picked up a mooring buoy and went up to the club for dinner. After five days we refueled, filled our water tanks, and left. Unfortunately, we were unable to get any propane for cooking and that was to plague us later. The propane tanks we had on board were either of French or English manufacture, so the fittings had different sizes than the Panamanian tanks.

After the excessive winds of the Atlantic and the Caribbean, it was strange to face a no-wind situation in the Pacific. Slowly, very slowly, we went beyond the channel markers of the canal and headed southwest to go beyond that part of Panama that sticks out. We certainly didn't make a fast passage. After three days we were out far enough to turn to the northwest, towards Costa Rica. We faced several dreadful rain storms with lots of thunder and lightning, but no wind, so it was slow. We had intended to enter Costa Rica at Golfito, but every cruiser was talking about a horrid official there who was harassing the crews of any boat that came in, so we avoided that. Instead we anchored off the small town of Quepos.

During the trip to Costa Rica I managed to catch an eighteen pound Mahi Mahi. This was the first fresh fish that we had in several weeks and it was great to eat fish again. All the water around Costa Rica was teeming with Mahi Mahi (dolphin fish) and we saw several bill fish. They were sail fish and marlin, I imagine. There were many other species of fish, but I didn't have time to investigate. In port we counted almost 100 charter boats that do nothing more than take a couple tourists out for the day, let him hook into a bill fish, bring it up to the boat, photograph and weigh it and turn it loose. A very sportsmanship way of satisfying the customer and also retaining a live fish in those waters.

The port captain and harbor master were gentlemen and the town was a delight. There was a superb restaurant there (George's) run by a man from San Francisco, California. There we had the finest filet mignon we have ever eaten. Then once again we topped off our fuel and water tanks and, after six days, moved north.

Up to this point if you had asked us to name our toughest passage we would've said the Red Sea, the English Channel, or the Bay of Biscay. Uh-uh! It's the passage north from Panama to San Diego. It's a monster! We headed way off shore so as to escape the reputed storms off the Gulf of Papagayo in Costa Rica and Gulf de Fonseca in Honduras. Even though we were 75 to 80 miles out we still had fierce winds. They were gale force and we had to put up the storm sails. Fortunately there was very little big boat traffic, but we could hear some yet couldn't see them. And that's always disturbing.

The further north we went the more confusing were the weather and sea conditions. There were long lines of ripples followed by a quiet spell and then more long lines of ripples. They were much like those we had experienced when leaving Bali so we weren't alarmed. Just puzzled as to what caused them.

After such strong winds, you're always relieved when it calms a little, but now it died completely. So we motored. We were going along at seven knots when we hit southward bound currents that pushed us back 30 miles. We went west, then east and in circles trying to get out of them, but had no luck. After four days I said that we were getting low on fuel so we were going to head for the 100 fathom line where he hoped the currents would be more favorable. Then we'd try to find a place to refuel.

Unfortunately, the 100 fathom line was very close to El Salvador and the nearest port was the town of Acajutla, El Salvador. We were desperately low on fuel. In case you don't remember, they had just ended a long civil war and were still unsettled. I said that they'd either welcome us or shoot us, so we agreed that we would go in and take our chances. When about two miles off shore Janet called on the VHF radio. Radio Acajutla answered and told us to go behind the breakwater and anchor with the fishing boats. We did. Two naval officers soon arrived in a *panga* (an open boat) and took our passports in to clear with the harbormaster.

Everyone in El Salvador was wonderful to us. There are no amenities for sail boats. The people were dirt poor because of the civil war and poverty abounded. However, the people were more than willing to share what they had. It was amazing to see the generosity of these people.

Radio Acajutla arranged for a small boat, again a *panga,* to bring us two 55 gallon drums of fuel. The *panga* was about 22 feet in length and had a 45 HP outboard engine. There was a crew of five young men, the oldest couldn't have been more than 20 years of age. They were a happy lot. Our languages did not mesh. We didn't speak Spanish and they no English. They had no siphoning gear at all. I furnished them a wrench to unscrew the lids, and gave them a piece of garden hose to siphon the fuel into jerry cans, which they handed to me and I poured it into the ships tanks. The oldest (the skipper) I'll call him Joe for lack of a name, did the siphoning. His first attempt was to get a mouthful of diesel but nothing more. He came up spitting and coughing. Whereupon the four crewmen thought that it was hilarious and laughed heartily. After a few tries Joe finally got the fuel to siphon, so we progressed to the end of the two barrels. The boys would laugh at the drop of a hat. What a jovial group.

My brother Jeff and I took our water jerry jugs to the fishermen's dock and filled them with water. This was no easy task as we had to manhandle each jug carefully down a twenty foot rickety ladder which I would have sworn would break on my next step. We had to make several trips to take on about eighty gallons of water.

A man from Radio Acajutla also picked me up and took me to the bank and the grocery store. Again, because of their civil war, there wasn't much to buy in the store, but I did manage to get some nice vegetables. Also one of the local fishermen kept bringing us ice. They were very nice people. This trip had been very fortuitous and we didn't get shot. On leaving we made a call to Radio Acajutla and thanked them for their hospitality and generosity and said that if they were ever in San Diego to look us up and gave them all the particulars. Their parting words were, "We will, we will."

When we left we once more went north west. We didn't want to stop in Guatemala for we had read of the thievery there and the rampant cholera, so our next port of call was to be Puerto Madeira on the southernmost tip of Mexico. We stayed off shore all the way up and headed in only when off the entrance to Puerto Madeira, Mexico.

And speaking of culture shock! You can't believe Puerto Madeira. It's just about twice as bad as you can imagine. The entering channel soon divides to left and right and we, unfortunately, took the left one. We motored past an incredibly dirty fishing village with bits and pieces of fish floating in the water. The stench of rotting fish was almost more than our nostrils could endure. The channel is a dead end and we asked a Mexican tugboat where to anchor. He pointed to a white buoy at one side and pantomimed dropping an anchor there. We anchored and the holding was excellent.

Jeff and I took our dinghy to the little village and walked through. It was an unbelievable sight. There were many fish that had yet to be cleaned and, I wouldn't have been surprised to learn, past the point of cleaning. The stink was nauseating and it was all we could do to breathe. We put a handkerchief over our noses but it didn't help. We hated the surroundings and after I cleared us in with the officials, we decided to go back to where the channel split and try the right fork.

On our starboard side, we motored past the Mexican naval base where we were eyed by the armed sentries in towers. Mexico was having a little civil war of its own with some rebels in the area. The naval base had some very zealous sentries on duty with machine guns pointing our way so we kept as far from them as possible. On our port side were dozens of rusting and derelict tuna boats. There were some that seemed to be in good enough condition to go out to sea, but they were few.

There was no place to tie up a dinghy when you went ashore. So with permission from one of the derelict tuna boats, we tied alongside to go ashore. It was a good deal as the crew watched and kept any thieves from stealing our dinghy. However, it was an obstacle course as there were three tuna boats tied side by side alongside of the dock. Two of the boats were being painted with red lead to keep the rust down. When we returned with several boxes and bags of groceries we found it near impossible to get back to our dinghy without getting red lead paint on us.

Beyond them was the anchorage and there were four other sailboats there. We joined them, grateful to be among other cruisers. Three of the boats, like us, were heading back to the States, and the fourth boat was going to Panama. They were a very sociable group of people and we enjoyed their company.

As three of us were going across the Gulf of Tehuantepec, we monitored all weather reports very carefully. After a short time (about four days), the radio said there was a four day wind window for crossing the dreaded Gulf. Those that were heading north soon departed.

For crossing Tehuantepec, the secret is to stay within the five fathom line. The wind whistles across in a funnel-like manner, becoming terribly fierce the further offshore you go. Five fathoms is 30 feet. Sometimes the depth finder brought us very close to shore. At times we would swear that we could step ashore without getting our feet wet. Close to shore you may get sandblasted, but there's no fetch to build up the waves. There are times you feel like you've got one foot on shore, but that's the only way to go. Hopefully you have a good depth finder. Even with that, you must keep a good watch and, as it's a one and a half to a two day trip, you're very glad when it's over.

The town of Salina Cruz is just on the edge of the Gulf and we pulled in to get some rest. We tied to the high dock behind the fire boat and had a pleasant stay. The bay is very dirty and the smells aren't very nice, but it was secure and safe. You check in at the end of the dock and the officials made it easy. Shopping was near by so we stocked up for our passage to Acapulco.

At this point we were very anxious to get home. The closer we got to San Diego the more anxious we became. Also Janet was quickly running out of her medications for her heart and diabetes. Because of that we hadn't planned to make many interim stops in Mexico and we didn't. So it was straight to Acapulco.

The entrance is very easy and we rounded the peninsula, motoring to the waters in front of the yacht club. We had been told to pick up one of the white, cone-shaped buoys in that area. They belong to the fishing boats and are only used by them in the winter, so we grabbed one. Oh, yes, they're free.

Checking in at Acapulco is a mess. You must go all over town, and it took me two days to get it done. The captain must ride a bus or expensive cab fare clear across town for one official. As all the cruisers complained about this, you'd think that the Mexican authorities would consolidate all their offices in one location. Probably not, as that's apparently too much to ask. But the shopping in the town was marvelous and there were some great restaurants.

We didn't stay long and were soon on our way to Zihuatenejo, about 180 miles north. It's really a beautiful little town and the holding in the anchorage was excellent. There isn't too much to see there, but it's peaceful and clean. We felt no regret at leaving, for we were going closer to home. And it was on to Manzanillo.

There we anchored in the main harbor among all the power and sail boats, as well as sports fishers, in the middle of the harbor. The holding wasn't good and we had to re-anchor, going closer to the jetty that had a Chinese restaurant on top of it. The owner of the restaurant gave me permission to tie our dinghy to it while I went ashore. Most convenient.

The passage across the open water to Cabo San Lucas was not pleasant. That damnable current again and very iffy winds. As we got closer to Cabo, the winds picked up to a Force 7-8 and the seas were no longer moderate. We could see the mooring buoys as we closed with the coast and we headed towards an open one. Most were taken by a variety of boats, many very close to the shore. That we didn't want, so we picked up one on the outer edge. They weren't free, but the price was reasonable and the fee was collected by a hotel employee.

At the dock in the marina I was able to arrange for fuel and water to fill our jerry jugs. I also met a professional boat deliverer who advised us to sail west for five days and then north for about eight days and we would be in San Diego. WRONG.

When we rounded the cape, those fierce currents caught us again, and even on a good beam reach, we began to be pushed south. After five days our GPS (electronic device to give geographical position) told us that we had not made much progress, so we turned on the diesel and headed north east for Magdalena Bay and the small village of San Carlos. Going through the narrow but well-marked channel to San Carlos was a bit hellish. There was no traffic and for that we were grateful. We went behind the huge dock at San Carlos and dropped the anchor well off the beach.

As Janet had run out of her heart medicine, I went down to the small clinic and tried to get some more for her. They didn't have what she had been taking, but provided a substitute. Unfortunately, all directions (there weren't many) were in Spanish so she didn't know how to take them. At this point she punted, but the medication was inadequate, to say the least. Her angina pains increased so I ordered her to bed, with only reading and bathroom privileges. Janet hated the confinement but bed was the only place where she endured less pain.

As we were unable to get any propane in Cabo, we soon ran out of it once we left San Carlos. In order to cook meals I had to use the "one pot" method and a blow torch. It worked, but slowly charred the burners on the galley stove. I had to set the pot somewhere safe and the stove was the only place for it. Then with my blow torch I would direct the flame to the bottom of the pot. As the regular burner was there it finally was charred beyond further use. I almost had an insurrection from my crew. I told them if they didn't like my cooking they could do it themselves. I will say it wasn't the best tasting stuff I had ever eaten. Under the circumstances the only thing I could do was to throw about three cans of different ingredients into a pot and heat it with the blow torch, and Yeck!

We tried to sail west again to get around Baja, but the currents kept sweeping us southeast, right back onto the rocks along the Baja coast. In desperation, we went into Turtle Bay to get some rest and some fuel, as we were really burning it up. It was at this point that we began to hear a dreadful noise from our shaft. I took a look and saw that it was whipping up and down. But we needed to run the engine to charge batteries and to get in and out of the anchorages, so we ran it, but not often.

Once again we headed due west to try and reach 117 degrees longitude. By going north on that course we'd go around Baja California and go straight to San Diego. Also we'd miss Cedros Island and that was a definite must. But we were fighting a losing battle. The wind was from the northwest, exactly where we wanted to go. So to make westing we had to go southwest which was taking us further from home. To make any northern progress we had to sail northeast which put us on the dirty brown edges of Mexico. Still, we had to get off the coast of Baja and, hopefully, out of the currents.

In the afternoon the wind picked up to Force 5 so I put up the Yankee. That increased our speed a little, yet we didn't make much forward progress. It was very depressing to have to sail away from San Diego, but there was no other choice. I figured that for each two miles traveled we made one mile to San Diego. That wasn't very encouraging. Several days showed that we had made only a mile or two to San Diego. "My Gawd!" I said to my crew. "At the rate we are going we won't get home until Christmas."

The wind would change direction with great frequency and we'd be shouting with joy one minute and down in the dumps the next. There was a fog bank on the horizon and we had only about mile to a mile and a half visibility, it was lousy weather.

I would run the engine in short spurts to charge the batteries and move us a little. But the noise was getting worse. Then Janet ran out of all her heart medication and I said I was going to run the engine until we were making a minimum of three knots or until the shaft broke and fell off.

Several days later, early in the morning, Janet called me and said that the bilge alarm had just gone off. I dashed below to find water coming up over the floor. I put Janet on the wheel and Jeff to bailing with the hand pump. I had to get to the source of the leak so I crawled over the refrigerator compressor and began to feel around in the bilges which were full of water. I discovered that the hose on the Pedro (a pipe through which the shaft runs and further is attached to the packing gland) was missing a stainless steel hose clamp and water was gushing in around the shaft faster than the bilge pump and Jeff could pump it out.

After several minutes I finally replaced the hose clamp and the surge of water ceased. All this time I had been working blindly in water over a foot deep. I said, "That was as close as we've ever come to sinking the boat." Water had been over knee deep in the boat and the boat was a mess. We threw all the sodden rugs overboard and got all of the debris out of the way. By removing all wet material and sopping up with a sponge it took months for the inside of the boat to dry out. As the packing gland was still leaking I set about fixing it. I took out all of the old packing and put in new. Now there's just an occasional drip from the packing gland. Thank goodness.

But we couldn't thank the wind for there was none. We made a lot of 360 degree turns and for several days progressed about 1 1/2 miles each day. And one day we drifted back 8 1/2 miles which didn't cheer us any. Neither did the 17 miles we drifted eastward one night.

The engine shaft really began to thunder and I took off the engine box to find the trouble. The trouble was that the fitting had broken at the flexible coupling and the engine was unusable to turn the propeller. Then the engine packed up all together. We could not get it started. Well, we still had the sails. The main and genny were up, but without being able to charge the batteries we'd soon lose our running lights. Not a pleasant prospect as we were still seeing very few merchant vessels around. And, while we never saw it, we didn't much care for our close proximity to Cedros Island.

We were still trying vainly to make westing and one day we made 13 miles. We were elated over that, but we're still a long way from home. The wind would pick up to Force 4 and then die away, but we averaged about 4 1/2 knots for a couple of hours. All under completely overcast skies. And another day we'd make 27 miles in westing (longitude) and lose 39 miles in latitude. The currents were pushing us south. For the next few days the elements just played with us. The seas would get very rough, then die down and the wind seemed to vary in speed and direction on an hourly basis. Then late one night all of us heard a loud bang like a gunshot. I looked all over the cockpit but couldn't see a thing in the dark. So I put on my safety harness and went forward. The shrouds and the stays were okay and I went back to the cockpit with a brighter light.

We have an inverted "Y" shaped back stay and I discovered that the back stay had snapped at the pivotal point of the "Y". I pulled down the Yankee pronto, set both running back stays, and left the trisail up as it also helped to hold the mast up. At that time the wind was from the north at Force 7 and gusting to Force 8. Again, the winds diminished and then increased, fluctuating all night.

With the back stay gone we have no HAM radio. We use the back stay as a random wire for our antenna. I attached an electric extension cord to the working end of the antenna and ran the loose end up to the second spreader on a halyard. Believe it or not we were in communications with a woman in Portland, Oregon, but couldn't receive any calls from our friends in San Diego.

I knew I would have to go up the mast to secure it with a line, and Janet was very apprehensive. She just knew she would never see me alive or in one piece again. I wasn't so keen on the idea myself, but as it was a lousy job, someone (meaning me) had to do it.

The seas were so rough and everything on deck and mast was very slippery. But I made it to the top of the mast with a lot of effort and help from Jeff pulling me up in a boatswain chair. Would you put your trust and faith in a seventy-eight year old man, not being very handy on deck and who could hardly tie a safe knot? Well, there wasn't much choice. After all, he was my brother, and there was only one other person and she wouldn't have been able with her heart condition.

With a great deal of trepidation and sheer determination, and yelling instructions at Jeff I went up the mast. It was as slippery as a greased pig from the dampness of all the inclement weather. We were in a force five wind and waves of about three to five feet. Just nice sailing weather. But at the top of the mast it was a Yo-Yo situation. I said to myself at the top, "I don't think I will ever make it safely back to the deck safely." There, at the top, I connected a shackle with 1/2" line attached that lead back to the cockpit.

I had more difficulty coming down than going up the mast. The mast was making a large arc back and forth. One minute I would be way out over the starboard side, the next minute I would be way out over the port side. All the time I was yelling at Jeff to lower slower or stop all together. Once about halfway down, my hands slipped. I could not retain my grip and swung much further out over the water. It would have been fun in the back yard in a tall tree swing but this was not the time and place for fun. Then, as the boat righted itself, I felt myself like in a swing, heading for the mast at good speed.

"Oh! Oh! I thought, "Here is where I decapitate my self, break my leg, or do something foolish." Well none of the above, luckily I was able to fend off with my feet, catch the mast securely and from that point on Jeff lowered me to the deck in safety. I just had to say a little silent prayer. "Thank You Lord!"

The line that I had attached at the top was then run through a block that I had attached in the cockpit, and I tightened the line down with a winch. Hopefully that would hold the mast upright until we got home. That night a freak wind of about Force 8-9 hit us for 3 or 4 minutes then calmed. I felt that a wind like that must have broken our back stay. It had and we were pushed back another 27 miles by headwinds and current.

Finally, on the 16th day out of Turtle Bay, we were able to get through on the HAM radio. We told them we were in a desperate situation and word was passed to friends. Then about 1800 that night a USCG plane flew over and dropped us a VHF radio for better reception. They told us that the CG cutter *Rush* would rendezvous with us at 0700 the following morning and to try and hold our course. We told them that we wouldn't abandon our boat and that we couldn't afford a commercial tow.

We did our best to stay on course 117 degrees longitude, but the currents pushed us away. The cutter *Rush* found us anyway. Then we got a call on the VHF to stand by as the cutter *Rush* would send a team of men over to help us. Two lieutenants and several enlisted men came aboard about 0730 and went right to work. One came aboard and wanted to see our shaft while two men began splicing the back stay, which was only a temporary job, but they did a superb job. The one looking at the shaft area said that it was a job that could only be completed on dry ground. As long as we could sail, we felt that we could still make it to San Diego.

Other men were bringing aboard jerry jugs full of water to fill our almost empty tanks and carrying boxes of food. They gave us a whole case of individual breakfast cereals, bread, fruit and 5 dozen eggs. They were very generous and proficient in their work and we did appreciate it very much. The small boats went back to the U.S. Coast Guard Cutter *Rush* and departed.

Then I downed the trisail and raised the main and Genny again. The wind was very light, again from the north west, and we weren't making more than two knots. And once again we were going back and forth on our same track. But we did have a bit of luck by contacting the tanker *Pt. Alaska* on the VHF. They contacted the Coast Guard in San Diego and would pass word to Southwestern Yacht Club. The Coast Guard would monitor our movements which weren't much.

Once we were able to get through on the HAM radio, but we couldn't make contact with any of the HAM nets. Our batteries were so low that we didn't dare try to run the radios for very long. We turned off all 12V switches except for the bilge pump, compass light and GPS. Those we needed. But we had no running lights for we weren't able to get the engine started to charge the batteries.

The wind would blow in spurts and then die again, so we made a lot of 360s. I took down the Genny as the gusts of wind were too strong for it, so we were trying to sail with just the main up. Then we had trouble getting our wind vane to hold. That's all we needed. But with some work it finally held although it didn't do much good as we were changing direction so often.

This was the very worst segment of our whole 11-year circumnavigation. You name it and it went wrong. I also had to repair a broken shroud and I did so with dog clips and lots of sweat and it seemed that I was getting very little sleep. I was continually repairing something necessary for the boat's operation or working for the welfare of the crew. Oh yes, the bob stay broke. What else could go wrong? This had to be repaired, but how? Finally I jury rigged a bob stay using flexible 1/4" wire and dog clips and tightened it as much as I dared. At the point of attaching the wire at the waterline I was thoroughly soaked by a wave. Well I probably needed that with all the sweating I'd been doing. Boating is just so much fun!

On our 22nd day a US Navy plane flew over us and Janet called them on the VHF. She told them we needed help. They said they would notify the Coast Guard in San Diego and would return to let us know what was happening. Just before dark they returned and said that another Coast Guard cutter would rendezvous with us the following morning at 0600. We were elated– help at last.

It was 0900 before the U. S. Coast Guard Cutter *Tybee* arrived. They also had trouble finding us, for again we had drifted. They sent a boarding party aboard to see if they could fix our engine or if we needed a tow to San Diego. With a broken shaft, no motor, batteries needed charging and contrary winds and currents the Coast Guard declared us a menace to navigation. We could abandon our boat or they would take us in tow. We opted for the latter.

They attached a bow line to us and began the 170 mile tow back to San Diego. Never has a boat looked more beautiful than the *Tybee* did that morning. But how ignominious to have to yell for help 170 miles from home after sailing 54,000 miles. However, without help we weren't making any headway and wouldn't be home 'til Christmas or later, or ever.

The tow began and we started to move in the right direction for the first time in a long time. The Coast Guard gave me a powerful handheld VHF so we could keep in communication with them and my job was to keep checking the tow line to see that it didn't come loose or chafe.

The tow was really very smooth and they towed us between 6 to 10 knots. The seas were also smooth on the northward trip, so we got lucky. At the speed we were going, they estimated that we would reach San Diego at 0900 the following morning. I talked to the Coast God (yes that is now what we call them) every hour so, once again, there was no sleep for me.

At dawn the following morning, we could see the coast of California although it was very foggy. We were very surprised at the number of vessels that came out to welcome us home. What a nice reception from so many good friends. There were horns honking, bells ringing, and loud shouts of "Welcome Home, Frank and Janet!"

When we pulled into the police dock to clear customs, we could see so many people standing back on the lawn. They were all waving at us and shouting our names. We wanted to see them so badly, but we couldn't until we were through with customs. But we called to them and told them to go over to the yacht club. By the way, the customs officer was wonderful. He asked Janet the value of everything we had purchased while overseas. She told him she didn't know for we'd been gone over 11 years. He thought for a moment and then said, "Write down $30.00." And that's what she did.

At that point two inflatable dinghies from Southwestern Yacht Club came along side and began pushing us across the yacht basin to the club and our slip. We could see so many people on the docks and across the front of the club was a huge sign that read "Welcome Home Frank and Janet". It was all almost overwhelming. But what was overwhelming was the number of people on the dock to catch our lines and greet us, complete with champagne. Besides sailing friends, there were cousins by the dozens, other long time friends, and many members of All Saints Episcopal Church. How good it was to see everyone and to feel their affection for us. It was quite an experience.

Janet said to me, "I now know why we had so much trouble coming up from Turtle Bay, we left there on a Friday." The old Portuguese superstition of never violating this tradition finally had some meaning and we vowed we would never let it happen again.

After 11 years, 1 month and 6 days we were home again, and it felt wonderful. It's great to be back in the land of plenty. Would we do it again? Yes, if we were 20 years younger.

Glossary

A CAPELLA: A singer without the aid of any instrumental accompaniment. I can't sing even with music.
AD MEASURER: A person measuring the length, breadth, and depth of a boat for registering with officials for purpose of documentation and fees.
AFT: Toward the stern, the blunty end of a boat.
ALBATROSS: The largest of all sea birds sometimes with a wingspan of 13 feet. These birds normally are hatched on Midway Island in the Pacific and fly many thousands of miles in the Southern Hemisphere. They are capable of soaring or gliding incredible distances without flapping their wings.
AMATEUR RADIO: See radio.
ANOPHELES: See mosquito.
ANCHOR: Many names–kedges, grapnels, sea anchor, mushroom, hook, to mention a few. A heavy metal device attached to a line or chain and dropped over the side of a vessel to restrain the movement of the boat.
ANCIENT MARINERS:. The Ancient Mariners I refer to is a group of people in San Diego with period sail boats built (I think) before 1952. This group consists of sloops, ketches, yawls, schooners have local and long distant races. Janet and I went on two of these races to Maui, Hawaii as associate members. These races were a great excuse to have a party at the end of the race.
BAKSHEESH: A bribe. Mainly in mideast countries.
BATTENED: A method of securing an object to keep it firmly in place.
BEAUFORT SCALE: A tabulation of figures indicating the strength of the wind (approximately).

Force	Wind	Knots	Force	Wind	Knots
0.	Calm	less than 1	7.	Moderate gale	28-33
1.	Light Air	1-3	8.	Fresh gale	34-40
2.	Light breeze	4-6	9.	Strong gale	41-47
3.	Gentle breeze	7-10	10.	Whole gale	48-55
4.	Moderate breeze	11-16	11.	Storm	56-65
5.	Fresh breeze	17-21	12.	Hurricane	over 65
6.	Strong breeze	22-27			

BILGE PUMP: A submersible pump placed in the lowest bilge area.
BINNACLE: A wood or other non-magnetic stand to hold a

compass. Generally has control cable for the excess water.
BOMMY: A mushroom-shaped coral reef, usually circular. The ones I have seen were only a few inches in diameter, to several feet across and variable in color.
BOW: The pointy (forward) end of the boat.
BUOY: Buoys are manufactured in many different shapes, colors, and are used for different purposes. They are used as floating beacons directing the mariner to position and passage. There are buoys that have bells, whistles, fog horns, and lights. There are other buoys used for mooring that come in different sizes, shapes, and colors.
CATAMARAN: A two hulled boat without a keel with cross structure of poles and netting, from very small racing catamarans to live-in quarters on larger boats. Usually it is sloop-rigged, but can have any number of masts and configuration of sails.
CHARTS: Maps of the sea, harbors and immediate shores showing the mariner many useful data, giving him information on depths, hazards, buoys and navigational devices etc. A chart at sea is like a road map to the landlubber. They are called various things in foreign countries. In France they are known by *cartes,* in Germany *karte.* The charts are very expensive and a prudent sailor will invest many thousands of dollars for a circumnavigation. If the sailor's pocketbook is handicapped he might try getting picture post cards of a harbor or port and cross his fingers behind his back and pray he makes it safely into the harbor (or stay at home).
CHECK VALVE: A rubberized piece of material, plastic, metal, or combination thereof, placed in a pipe to allow fluid to flow in one direction only.
CUTTER RIG: A cutter rigged boat generally has the mast stepped a little further aft and will have two or more forestays. It will generally be narrower and a deeper draft than a sloop. Normally it will fly a combination of sails depending on the direction of wind etc.
DACRON: A man made synthetic material which is used in manufacturing lines (Ropes to landlubbers) and sails. Sails can be made of very light Dacron (say 2 oz.) used for spinnakers, ghosters, or other very large sails used in very light winds. For winds of more than 8 or 10 knots, Dacron sails of heavier material should be used for endurance. I've used my 4 oz. Main and Jibs, in winds of 15 to 20 knots. My 8 oz. Dacron Main, Jib, and Yankee come to play in 20 to 35 knot winds. Over 35 knots and my 12 oz. Storm Staysail, Jib

or Trisail goes up. Both sails and lines have very little stretch or give so will hold shape and resists mildew.

DEAD RECKONING (D.R.): Some of our early barnstorming airplane pilots were known to fly by the seat of their pants. Dead Reckoning or DR as sailors term it, is essentially the same thing only navigating a boat. The sailor calculates his speed, drift, speed of currents and its effect as well as compass errors and course(s) steered to determine his geographical position without the aid of any celestial observation. This is a a real test of the navigator's skill but should only be relied upon as a secondary measure to electronic satellite fixes (GPS) or actual sextant observations calculated to geographical position and/or other devices that will give true fixes.

DOG CLIPS: Metal fasteners that clamp two wires together so tightly the wires do not slip.

EPIRB: Emergency, Position, Indicating, Radio Beacon. A very low frequency radio (usually line of sight) emitting an SOS, Mayday or Distress signal.

EL NIÑO: A warming of currents off the coast of Peru and Ecuador usually in late December which may cause terrible weather effects to areas as far as Australia and even Indonesia. The weather effects can last six months or longer. As late as June/July on our trip to Hawaii in 1983, the El Niño was still in effect and not once did we see the sun, planet or any heavenly bodies that we could take a sextant shot. There was no animal life to be seen. Rather spooky.

FETE: A festive day of celebration in France held on Bastille Day or the 14th of July, that lasts for one day. In French Society Islands (Bora Bora where we were) the Fete lasted many days. Three different villages participated making their own unique costumes, preparing and practicing three songs, one of which had to be sung by the other two villages. There was native dances, drum beating and other acts. It was a beautiful entertainment of three days and nights.

FLEXIBLE COUPLING: A heavy thick plastic and metal shaped material fitted between the flange of the transmission shaft and the flange attached to the shaft. This allows for better alignment of the shaft.

GALE: See Velocity of wind.

GENOA: Nicknamed guinny or jenny. This is a large overlapping sail that sheets well aft of the mainmast. Our jenny was a 140 % made of 4 oz. dacron and our best pulling sail in winds up to 20 knots.

GESTUNKEN: My German friend Manny's description of what he thought of the Russians. 'Nuff explanation.

GYBE also **JIBE**: A variation in the spelling. This term refers to changing tacks by running off before the wind. In simpler terms when we were disabled by not having the use of our main rudder, we could not bring our bow across the wind when tacking. Therefore on a starboard tack to port tack, we would continue going to port until our stern crossed the wind and we were able to take up a port tack. We had to make sure the main was sheeted in tight or firmly secured before such a maneuver. From a port tack to starboard tack we did the opposite maneuver.

GPS: An electronic instrument that gave us latitude and longitude, speed, course, way points, etc., and served me a beer when I was thirsty. I'm kidding of course. A very accurate instrument.

GUNK HOLE, The Mariner Dictionary by Gershom Bradford copyright 1972 defines Gunk Hole as a small narrow channel dangerous to navigate owing to current and to numerous rocks and ledges. A small anchorage, usually shallow. Gunk holing adds much interest and pleasure for shoal draft boatmen. I agree wholeheartedly with all. We personally would never anchor in any place that was dangerous or we thought our anchor would not hold, and generally the spot to be sheltered from wind or currents. We found many safe Gunk Holes and had intense pleasure on the French Riviera.

GUNWALE (GUNNEL): A rail (fibre glass on my boat) going around the boat that is about even with my deck and supports my stanchions for my lifelines.

HALYARD (HALLIARD): line used in hoisting sails to the desired height of the mast.

HEAVENLY BODIES: The Sun, Planets, Constellations, Stars and Marilyn Monroe. Let's face it. It is pretty much of a man's world.

HEBERWERK LOCK: A modern day miracle of German engineering. See Chapter 9 for details.

HIGH PRESSURE: An atmospheric condition which is abnormal, causing the barometer to rise. During this condition the winds usually cease, the seas become flat, and you sit and bob like a cork in a bathtub of water. This is the time to get out your rubber ducky.

HURRICANE: This is a storm with velocity of 65 knots or better sometimes going much higher than 100 knots, cyclonic in nature, usually in a counterclockwise motion.

Generally applies to those violent agitations over the West Indies. Typhoon is the name given to similar disturbances occurring in the East Indies; the motion is in a clockwise movement. The hurricane winds we were in (see Chapter 3) were not circular as the normal hurricane or typhoon, but in a straight line. Southerly Busters have straight lined winds, but usually are less than 60 knots.

JETTY: A breakwater usually to hold currents of water or divert water. In rare cases boats are tied bow to the jetty for mooring or in some cases used as a dock, pier or quay.

KETCH: A two masted rig, the foremast being the tallest. The mizzen mast is the shorter after mast,

KNOCKDOWN: The boat is thrown on beams-end by strong gusts of winds, a rogue wave, or a combination of both.

KNOT: The nautical term refers to measure of speed, not one of distance. A nautical mile is equal to 6,076.1 feet. In navigation 6000 feet and 2000 yards are usually used.

LATITUDE: Latitude is an arbitrary line(s) shown on a world globe running east and west from the north pole to the south pole and is the angular distance, measured north or south of the equator, of a point of the earth's surface, expressed in degrees. A minute of latitude is equal to one nautical mile or 6,076.1 feet. San Diego is located roughly at 32 degrees latitude.

LEEWARD: To the lee, or away from the wind, especially if you are going to be seasick.

LES TRUCK: A truck converted and adapted as a bus in the French Society Islands.

LIFE LINES: These are lines made of various materials on different boats. Some are stainless steel, some are wood or other material, On my boat they are of stainless steel wire covered by a plastic coating and supported by stanchions. These are not to be leaned on but are a measure of safety in keeping a person from being washed overboard. We hope– we hate wet crewmen.

LIFE RAFT: This is generally a circular boat with air tanks to quickly inflate it. It has deep rubberized compartments to help steady the boat and keep it from drifting too fast. Covered by a canopy to shield a person from sun and elements. Also it has a few provisions and water to keep a person alive until rescued a few days later after his ship has sunk.

LOCK: A lock is an enclosed body of water with a gate at each end. A ship enters the downside. The gate closes, water begins to enter the dock and raises the ship to next level higher. The opposite gate he entered opens and the ship goes into another lock or level of water he can safely navigate. In going down the operation is reversed.

LONGITUDE: The position of a ship or person east or west from the meridian of Greenwich (0 degrees through 180 degrees, and is the distance in degrees, minutes and seconds. Longitudinal lines run north and south from the North Pole to the South Pole. San Diego California is roughly 117 degrees longitude.

LOW PRESSURE: An atmospheric condition of low or light pressure causing the barometer to drop. This low pressure is the indication of of winds, and lousy weather, or rain the farmers need.

MAHI MAHI: A dolphin fish. A true fish and not related in the least to a dolphin or porpoise. Mahi Mahi is delicious eating.

MELTEMI: A wind normally gale force that blows northeasterly in the Mediterranean. These winds are very fierce at times and do lots of damage to property, boats and people.

MONSOON: Seasonal winds, rains and generally bad weather.

MOORING: There are several ways that a boat is moored. It is truly moored when the ship has a bow and a stern anchor firmly down. However, if tied to a mooring buoy, it is said that she is moored. Firmly tied to a dock, quay, pier, slip, etc., is also mooring.

NAUTICAL: A term pertaining to ships and navigation (not a naughty boy).

NAUTICAL MILE: A nautical mile equals 6,076.1 feet.

NEPTUNE: A mythical god of the sea.

NETS, NET CONTROL: These are control stations set at various places around the world to monitor Amateur Radio. The Pacific Net was located in Washington State in June 83 to January 84, maybe longer. I believe they were assisted by an operator in Hawaii. Tony's net was located in New Caledonia and New Zealand. Rowdy's net was out of Hong Kong. They specified they would be on a given frequency at a certain time. Their agenda would start with health and emergencies, If none, they would ask mariners to report as called by code name to report, location, weather, winds problems, moral factors etc. Almost daily a boat had a maintenance problem and another boat could help solve his problem. Amateur Radio (Ham) is God's gift to the mariner.

PACKING GLAND: A heavy fabricated rubberized material attached by hose clamps to the pedro and the other end attached to the gland by a second hose clamp. The gland holding the packing around the shaft was then tightened by threaded metal sleeve or nut. When tightened sufficiently it would only allow a drip per minute or as desired to keep the gland and shaft lubricated.

PANGA: An open boat 20-24 feet in length, powered usually by a 45 H.P. outboard motor and used as a work or fishing boat in Mexico and Central America.

PEDRO or SHAFT TUBE: A permanent fixture in the boat where the shaft emerges through the hull to be affixed to a propeller.

PENICHES: These are commercial river or canal barges. They had to be a maximum of 20 feet on specified canals with locks of specified sizes. Of course larger in width if they traveled on rivers or locks of wider widths. The peniches usually were a minimum of fifty feet in length up to several hundred in length. They were of very shallow draft and could carry mucho cargo.

PLUMERIA: A flowering shrub and/or tree, with beautiful plumes, colors, and odor. Most leis (flower necklaces) are made entirely of Plumeria.

POSEIDON: A mythical god of the sea.

PORT: The left side of the boat when you face forward toward the pointy end. Also a harbor where ships go in and out. Also an opening in the side for air and light (windows to a land lubber), or in olden days gun ports.

PORT TACK: Sailing with the wind blowing over the port or left side of the boat.

QUAY: Pronounced key. Quays are docks, piers, etc., and mainly known in Europe.

RADIOS: **1. VHF**–This is a very high frequency radio, supposedly a line of sight. However, during one broadcast we made, there was a freak skip and the transmission went over 400 miles. **2. Amateur Radio (HAM)** –This radio is used world wide for receiving and transmitting. A very important piece of equipment that all sailors should have. **3. EPIRB**– emergency positioning indicating radio beacon. A line of sight radios emitting emergency signals of SOS, Mayday, or distress signal.

RADIO NETS, See **NETS, NET CONTROL.**

RIGGING: Wire ropes usually made of stainless steel, or galvanized steel. These are called stays (running fore and aft) and shrouds on port and starboard, holding the mast in vertical position. All this is called the standing rigging.

Running rigging is Dacron, manila, nylon, or hemp materials that control the sails.

ROACH COACH: These coaches in Tahiti were privately owned businesses on the water front selling various foods: steak and chips, spaghetti and meat balls, crepes, ice cream, etc., for a very reasonable price. At the time we were there, any of the forgoing would sell for $3.00US or less. I never saw a roach on any of them. A cheap and good place to eat.

SAFETY HARNESS: A heavy webbing material usually made of Nylon or Dacron affixed to a person with a line and quick release hook to enable a crew member to hook on quickly almost any where on the boat to keep him safely and securely aboard. A rigid rule on my boat–wear safety harness at any time on deck; we hate wet crewman that have been dunked, besides they drink too much coffee to warm up.

SATNAV: An archaic piece of electronic equipment that went out the door when the new GPS came in. It would give us our geographical position about once in an hour's time, but in the South Pacific we would get readings maybe once in 12- some hours.

SCHOONER: A two masted boat with the shorter spar (mast) forward and used a number of sails.

SEXTANT: An instrument to measure altitude from the boat to heavenly bodies and horizontal angles between landmarks to establish a fix.

SHEETS: These are various size lines and/or colors to control the sails.

SHOCK CORD: See Bungy.

SHROUD: See Rigging.

SIGNAL FLAGS: A set of signal flags consists of alphabetical and numbered flags plus a few repeat flags for signaling another boat or shore with various messages.

SLOOP: A single masted boat that flies two sails, a main sail and one header sail forward.

SPACE A: This term is mainly used by the U.S. Air Force to denote space available on a military air plane. Because I am retired from the military I am afforded the privilege to fly if a seat is available.

SQUALL: A sudden gust of wind sometimes accompanied by rain, sleet or snow with a force of 7 or better on the Beaufort Scale.

STARBOARD: The right side of the boat when you face forward to the pointy end.

STAYS: See Rigging.

STERN: The aft or blunty end of the boat.
STORM: See Beaufort Scale.
SOUTHERLY BUSTERS: Very strong and sudden winds, of Force 8 or better on the Beaufort Scale, off the coast of Australia.
TACK: Sailing with the wind on one side of the boat. Tack is also to bring the bow across the wind to the other side,
TOPLESS WOMEN: Yeah! Yeah! I have a coffee cup with the words, "Over the hill and still playing around."
TRANSPAC RACE: There were several (maybe still going) Transpac races. One Transpac race was from Vancouver, British Columbia to Honolulu. Another from Los Angeles to Honolulu. Janet and I made two Transpac races with the Ancient Mariners back in the 70s.
TRANSOM: The aft part of the boat hull.
TROPICAL CONVERGENCE: Unusual winds of varying strengths that changes many degrees continually in a very short time.
TROPICAL DEPRESSION: An area of low pressure atmospheric conditions.
VHF: See Radio.
WEATHER FAX: An electronic instrument that that receive radio signals of weather for various areas and can chart them on graphs.
WINDVANE: A device attached to the stern that when the conditions are right and the vane is set will steer the boat automatically as long as the wind remains steady.
WINDWARD: Wind blowing toward the boat. Never spit to windward, It will come back at you.
WANSEE: A large lake almost in the center of Berlin, Germany.
WASSER POLIZE: Water police in Germany.
YARMULKE: A skull cap the Jewish people wear, especially at prayers, blessings and ceremonies.

A Brief History and Description of the *Isle of Barra*

The sailing yacht, *Isle of Barra*, is named after the author's ancestral home in Scotland, in the Outer Hebrides. The hull and deck were manufactured by Yorktown Yachts in Long Beach, California, in 1972. In January 1973 it was trucked to the Yorktown yard in San Diego, behind the Sports Arena, for finishing all interior work. In 1975 it was taken to the old Kettenburg Yard for rigging and completion and then motored to Southwestern Yacht Club. Description as follows:

Documentation No. 568683
Gross tonnage	12 tons
Net tonnage	11 tons
Length	39.1 feet
Breadth	11.9 feet
Depth	5.5 feet
Ballast	9,500 lbs. lead/concrete
Hull material	FRP
Propelled	Perkins 4108 diesel

It is a cutter with the following rigging:
Sails	2 Mainsails
	1 4 oz. Dacron
	1 8 oz. Dacron
	1 Genoa 4 oz. Dacron
	1 Jib 4 oz. Dacron
	1 Yankie 8 oz. Dacron
	1 Storm Staysail 12 oz. Dacron
	1 Storm Jib 12 oz. Dacron
	1 Storm Trisail 12 oz. Dacron
Fuel (diesel)	2 54 gal. tanks 40 gals Jerry jugs on deck
Water	2 20 gal. tanks under cockpit
	1 40 gal. tank in forepeak
	Several jerry jugs on deck

167 Electronic equipment has been changed many times over the years. Currently using a GPS, 1 permanent and 2 hand-held VHF radios, plus an amateur radio with a general license with code letters (call sign) N6EZI. We had many other pieces of equipment, but few were used (or used for long) due to climatic conditions causing deterioration of wiring and components.

One of the most important items besides the compass and the GPS is our windvane, nicknamed Bruce. As long as the wind was steady at 5 knots or more, it would hold the course steadier than a human.

On the cruise, we bought approximately $8,000 worth of charts.

Janet and Frank McNeill

Janet was born September 1, 1926, in Indiana. Since she came to California when she was two months old, she claimed to be a native. She attended local schools, getting straight "A"s in all subjects without taking a book home for homework. At U.C.S.D and S.D.S.U., she earned enough credits for a master's degree had she cared to apply for one. She thought it would be useless in her chosen career as wife, mother, boat builder, and sailor. She found the knowledge helpful, though, in her volunteer duties at Scripps Oceanography Institute and as a docent at various museums in Balboa Park.

Frank was born in Colorado January 14, 1921. He was a junior in high school when he dropped out to join the U. S. Marine Corps in 1939. During his tour in the Marines he went to many service schools and took correspondence courses. Midway through his twenty-year service he received a much coveted high school diploma.

After his retirement from the Marine Corps, he attended San Diego Junior College and studied business administration at San Diego State University. During this time, he worked full time at various medical clinics and hospitals, which led to his career as Senior Buyer for the University Hospital Medical Center. He retired for good in 1982.

Janet met Frank at a church social function in 1942, when he was a marine. It was love at first sight, but Frank was shocked to learn that Janet was only fifteen and tried to stay away. That proved to be impossible, and the couple was married on January 5, 1943, a year to the day after they had met.

They embarked on a journey through life, ending after fifty-four years with Janet's death in New South Wales, Australia, on March 29, 1997.